COMBAT SHAOLIN

COMBAT SHAOLIN

Authors:
Gary Tang,
Albert Loui,
and Brian Klingborg

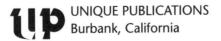
UNIQUE PUBLICATIONS
Burbank, California

First published in 2003 by Unique Publications.

Library of Congress Catalog Number: 2002155297
ISBN: 0-86568-215-1

Unique Publications
4201 Vanowen Place
Burbank, CA 91505
(800) 332–3330
First edition
05 04 1 3 5 7 9 10 8 6 4 2

Printed in the United States of America.

Editor: Dave Cater
Design: Patrick Gross
Cover Design: George Chen

ACKNOWLEDGEMENTS

Gary Tang: I'd like to thank Kevin Lew, Andreas Moppin, Ky Nguyen, Sabatian Nguyen, Sophia Nguyen, Kenneth Leung, Alfred Leung, C.K. Lee, Julie Ong (for her help with the photo sessions), Kevin Lew (for helping to prepare the photo studio), Kin O. Leung (for Chinese consulting). Gabriel Tang, my 7-year-old son, and Christina Shea, my wife, helped with the Chinese during the early stage of my writing.

Albert Loui: I would like to thank Lai Sifu for investing time and trust in him—the duties and responsibilities placed on his shoulders is of a filial sort, and it is a great honor to learn from such an immensely talented master.

Brian: This one is for Mom and Dad.

From left to right: Lillian Chow, authors Gary Tang and Albert Loui, and Kevin Chin.

Note on Chinese Usage

Several forces produced the gradual diaspora of Chinese kung-fu practitioners to the Americas (and points beyond) from the 1950s to the 1970s. One of the major root factors was the establishment of the Communist government in 1949, which sparked an exodus of martial talent to Hong Kong that eventually trickled to the West. Since the vast majority of these masters were originally from the Kwangtung province in southern China, the "lingua franca" of kung-fu is the Cantonese dialect. As such, we endeavor to use the Yale system of Cantonese Romanization to represent names and terminology. Geographical locations are a principal exception (i.e., "Kwangtung" versus "Guangdong"). When appropriate, Mandarin Romanization occurs and in this text is represented in the Wade-Giles system (versus Pinyin).

TABLE OF CONTENTS

FOREWORD

Let's begin by posing a question: Why are you attracted to the Chinese martial arts? Are you searching for a practical form of self-defense? Are you seeking a way to improve your health and increase longevity? Are you hoping to achieve a closer bond between your body and mind? Or is it just that you think the martial arts are good fun? Perhaps you are motivated by all of the above. The bottom line is that there are as many reasons for learning the martial arts as there are students practicing them.

The luxury of our relatively peaceful times is such that we are free to view the martial arts any way we like—as a form of exercise, a holistic endeavor, or simply as entertainment. Although yesterday's masters were interested in health and longevity, for them the martial arts were geared first and foremost toward preparing for physical combat.

Over the centuries, many martial systems have lost some of their practical effectiveness because of various factors, including: imperfect transmission between generations; the refusal of some masters to reveal their most-prized techniques; or the death of a master before the entire system could be passed down. But, without exception, the dozens of Chinese martial arts currently being practiced around the globe were originally conceived with combat in mind.

That's not to say the martial arts should ignore the pursuit of better health, longer life and mental well-being. Achieving such goals is part and parcel of the martial arts experience, and they tend to become increasingly important as the practitioner enters his "golden years." In fact, most martial arts curriculums are usually complemented with a variety of physical and mental exercises (often informally referred to as "chi kung"), whose sole purpose is to improve the quality of life. Yet, even in these modern times, when the mindset of most martial arts students is far different from that of their predecessors, a martial art cannot really be considered "martial" if it disregards the combat application of its techniques.

The potential for violence in the martial arts has always been balanced with a philosophy of Wu Te, or "Martial Virtue," without which no martial artist's training was considered complete. Some traditional masters even asserted that if two men met in combat, the more virtuous fighter was assured victory. This is a rather naïve view, as both ancient and more-recent history have shown that martial excellence and thuggish behavior are not mutually exclusive. Nevertheless, it should be emphasized that while the martial arts are, by definition, systems designed for physical combat, fighting is not the essence of a martial artist, and no true master would ever unleash his skills indiscriminately or capriciously.

When it comes to unarmed physical combat, the Chinese classics refer to four main skills:

1. *Ta (striking)*—This includes any attack using the fist, open hand, fingers, elbows or any part of the arms.
2. *T'i (kicking)*—Any attack that makes use of the legs, knees or feet.
3. *Ch'in Na (locking, seizing, striking vital points, breaking)*— Locking is defined as moving the joints contrary to their natural range of motion; Seizing is defined as grasping or squeezing vital points of the body, causing a disruption of energy flow[1]; Striking vital points is often referred to as Dim Mak (in Mandarin, Tien Hsueh) in martial arts publications; Breaking means to fracture a bone.
4. *Shuai (throwing)*—Any method that causes your opponent to fall to the ground; includes sweeping, tripping and various types of takedowns and throws.

---

1. Zhao Da Yuan, *Practical Chin Na, A detailed analysis of the art of seizing and locking,* (Highview Press, 1993).

Combat Shaolin focuses on a two-person form taken from the Northern Shaolin curriculum. All the above skills are represented in this form. In more traditional times, forms were practiced to give students a feeling for the give and take of physical combat, as well as a means of drilling many of Northern Shaolin's key fighting techniques in a safe, yet realistic manner. With an experienced partner, this form would allow a student to unleash full power kicks, strikes, grappling moves and throws, and to defend against the same kinds of attacks when it was his partner's turn to take the offensive.

Of course, one cannot expect to learn to fight simply by practicing a form. A real mastery of physical combat requires years of specific drills; training with a partner using unrehearsed exchanges of techniques; striking and kicking heavy bags and other types of practice equipment; learning to absorb and recover from actual full-power attacks; and special mental preparation. But learning and performing this two-person form is a worthwhile adjunct to these other kinds of activities. For one thing, students of the traditional arts know that it is sometimes difficult to extract the true application of a combat technique from a one-person form; but in the case of a two-person form, the application (or, at least, one possible application) is right there, front and center, waiting for you to come along and collect it. To apply these applications in an unrehearsed setting still requires a great deal of analysis and practice, but at least the two-person form will provide a taste of how Northern Shaolin techniques are used in a combat situation.

The two-person form presented in this book comes directly from master Lai Hung, one of the greatest living treasures of the Chinese martial arts. A lineage holder in both the Northern Shaolin and the Choy Lay Fut systems, Lai Hung is primarily known as one of kung-fu's fiercest full-contact fighters. Even after more than four decades of practice, Lai Hung still finds the two-person form both enjoyable and educational. The authors hope you will find the contents of the following pages equally enjoyable and educational.

Chapter 1
NORTHERN SHAOLIN
DEFINED

In modern times, the term "Northern Shaolin" (Pei Shao Lin, as rendered in Mandarin, or Buk Sil Lam in Cantonese) has been used indiscriminately to refer to any Chinese martial art thought to have originated in the Shaolin Temple in Honan province. While this is not inaccurate in a literal sense, "Northern Shaolin", at least when used as a proper noun, is a distinct Chinese martial system with a specific curriculum. There are variations in the curriculum from school to school, because some instructors choose to add or delete certain auxiliary forms, but the essence of Northern Shaolin is contained in its ten core forms:

1. *Open the Gate (K'ai Men/Hoi Mun)*
2. *Lead the Way (Ling Lu/Ling Lou)*
3. *Astride the Horse (Zuo Ma/Cho Ma)*
4. *Pierce the Heart (Ch'uan Hsin/Chyun Sam)*
5. *Martial Technique (Wu Yi/Mou Ngai)*
6. *Short-Distance Fighting (Tuan Ta/Dyun Da)*
7. *Plum Flower Moves (Mei Hua/Mui Fa)*
8. *Leaping Strides (Pa Pu/Bat Bou)*
9. *Linked Moves (Lian Huan/Lin Waan)*
10. *Skilled Method (Shih Fa/Sik Faat)*

There are also a wide variety of weapons forms available in the Northern Shaolin curriculum. The primary weapons taught are the staff, spear, saber and broadsword. Other common weapons forms include the double hook swords, long handled knife, halberd, nine-section chain whip, and three-section staff. And there's also the two-person sparring form that is the primary topic of this book (known in Cantonese as Buk Siu Lam Yi Yan Deui Chaak).

Essentially a long-range style, Northern Shaolin seeks to keep opponents at the range of a kick or an extended strike, although it should also be mentioned there are a variety of close-range fighting techniques within the style. Northern Shaolin practitioners are chiefly famous for their kicking skills. The primary kicks of the style include, a straight front kick with the heel or ball of the foot; a front or round kick using the instep or shin; a low side kick; inside and outside crescent kicks; sweeping kicks; jumping front and side kicks; and a jumping spinning tornado kick. Hand techniques include, straight punches (mainly using an upright fist); backfists; hammmerfists; uppercuts; hooking punches; and finger and palm strikes. In terms of throws, Northern Shaolin incorporates forward and backward sweeps, leg hooking techniques, and several body throws that make use of the horse stance when moving in and uprooting an opponent. There are also numerous chin na skills in the Northern Shaolin curriculum.

Chapter 2
HISTORY OF NORTHERN SHAOLIN

The exact origin of the Northern Shaolin style is unknown. There are no written documents that trace the lineage of the style from its inception to the present day. Most modern Northern Shaolin schools simply rely on a family tree that has been passed down—in some cases orally—from generation to generation. As a result, different Northern Shaolin schools, which teach essentially the same basic curriculum, do not always pay homage to the same set of ancestors. Some of this discrepancy may be the result of language; there are dozens of dialects spoken in China, and a single master may have had disciples who hailed from many different provinces. Each of these disciples, when rendering the master's name in his own dialect, would pronounce it differently. Also, many of the martial artists of old were not educated, so they did not have the means to provide a written family tree, thus clearing up any potential confusion regarding ancestral names. Whatever the reasons, the end result is that Northern Shaolin's historical development remains a matter of some debate.

One of the more probable theories regarding Northern Shaolin's roots, however, is that the style was the joint effort of several monks, or even successive generations of monks, living at the Shaolin Temple in Honan province. These monks are said to have combined combat techniques from the main martial arts systems, which were practiced at the Temple. In the early 18th century, a lay disciple of the Shaolin Temple (a lay disciple is someone who studied the martial arts and/or Buddhism at the Temple, but was not ordained as a monk), named Kan Feng-chih brought the Northern Shaolin system out of the temple and into the broader world. From Kan Feng-chih, the system passed to Wan Peng-ts'ai, and then successively to Yen Te-kung, Yen San-sen, Yen Chi-wen, and finally to Ku Ju-chang[2]. During this passage from master to master, Northern Shaolin migrated from Honan province to Shantung province and eventually, under the guidance of Ku Ju-chang, to Kwangtung province. Ku's disciples spread the style to Hong Kong, and their disciples introduced Northern Shaolin to the rest of the world.

Fig. 2.1: Ku Ju-chang

The history of Northern Shaolin becomes more easily verifiable when the towering figure of Ku Ju-chang (Fig. 2.1) enters the scene. Some people even believe that Ku himself created the ten core forms from a variety of martial arts systems he studied. Others believe that the forms have too much of an essential "Shaolin Temple" flavor for Ku to have invented them himself (since Ku never actually studied at the Shaolin Temple). All agree, however, that Ku put the final stamp on the Northern Shaolin system practiced today.

2. Ching, Gene, *Bak Sil Lum vs. Shaolin Temple #2: Who's got the real Shaolin kung fu,* (Kungfu Magazine, 2001).

In many ways, Ku Ju-chang's biography resembles one of the kung-fu adventure novels of old that spawned many of the legends surrounding notable martial artists such as Wong Fei-hung. He was born in 1893 or 1894 in Chiangsu province. His father, Ku Li-chih, was a martial arts expert who made his living by providing security for merchants traveling with their goods through the bandit-infested roads leading to and from the city of Nanking. It is said that Ku Li-chih was illiterate, which was not an uncommon condition at that time. When he had a son, Ku Yu-men, he decided that the child would concentrate on academics rather than martial arts. However, he also wanted one of his heirs to continue the family business, so when he had a second son, Ku Ju-chang, he resolved that the boy would learn martial arts as well as reading and writing. Before Ku Ju-chang reached his teens, Ku Li-chih taught him the T'an-t'ui system of which he was a master. Unfortunately, as was common in those days, Ku Li-chih took ill and died prematurely. Ku Ju-chang was about 14 when his father died.

At some point, the elder Ku had struck up a friendship with a man named Yen Chi-wen, who at the time resided in Shantung province. Like Ku Li-chih, Yen was involved in the security business. He was also the inheritor of the Northern Shaolin style. Although the details are a bit hazy, it appears that the Northern Shaolin style was brought out of the Shaolin Temple by Kan Feng-chih and passed from master to master until it was entrusted to the Yen family. From there, it was passed from father to son and apparently used as the preferred style for the Yen security business. When he realized his death was imminent, Ku Li-chih advised his son to seek out Yen Chi-wen for further martial arts instruction.

When he was around 16, Ku Ju-chang made the long journey to Shantung province. When he appeared on Yen Chi-wen's doorstep, he was immediately accepted as part of the Yen family (some historians refer to Yen as Ku's uncle, but it's most likely that Yen was considered an uncle by virtue of his close relationship with Ku's father, rather than by blood or marriage). By most accounts, Ku studied with Yen for 11 years. He is said to have learned the same ten core forms (plus the one two-person sparring form, many weapons forms and probably some additional miscellaneous forms) practiced today by Northern Shaolin students. He also received from Yen Chi-wen the famous iron palm and golden bell (iron body) techniques that later brought him such enormous fame (Figs. 2.2, 2.3 and 2.4). After mastering Yen Chi-wen's curriculum, Ku Ju-chang spent some time traveling around China, gaining what martial arts knowledge he could from other sources.

There is an oft-told story that illustrates the heroic status Ku Ju-chang was accorded by later generations. The story seems somewhat embellished, but there are eyewitness and newspaper accounts verifying that the event occurred. As the tale goes, in 1925 or 1931, depending upon the source, a Russian circus came to town. The circus promoters offered a large sum of money to anyone who could withstand three kicks from its star attraction, a giant war-horse. As anyone who has experience with horses knows, this was quite a serious challenge: a horse's kick can easily kill a human. Ku Ju-chang agreed to try, with the stipulation that he would be allowed strike the horse in return if he

Fig. 2.2: Ku Ju-chang demonstrating his iron palm technique.

survived the kicks. On the appointed day, Ku Ju-chang arrived, performed a variety of chi kung exercises as a warm-up, then went on to take three of the horse's full-power kicks directly to his chest. After recovering from the last kick, Ku Ju-chang gave the horse a

Fig. 2.3: Ku Ju-chang with a car parked on his abdomen.

Fig. 2.4: Ku Ju-chang demonstrating his iron body technique.

palm slap on its hindquarters. The horse immediately fell dead. An autopsy revealed that many of the horse's internal organs had been ruptured.

Ku Ju-chang's fame was truly cemented in 1928 when he took part in a national martial arts tournament sponsored by the Chinese government. At the time, the government was hoping to use the Chinese martial arts as a means to unite the increasingly fragmented and beleaguered country. The tournament, perhaps the largest ever held in China up to that time, featured both forms and fighting competition. By all accounts, there were few rules governing the combat other than the barring of eye, throat or groin attacks. The fights were unrestrained and many injuries resulted. Ku Ju-chang beat the two opponents he faced. Soon after his second victory, the tournament organizers decided to halt the fighting competition, lest the greatest masters in the country ended up killing or seriously harming one another! Depending on the source, including Ku Ju-chang, the either 13 or 15 masters who were undefeated at the time the tournament was halted were declared champions of the fighting competition.

In the wake of the tournament, Ku Ju-chang and four other masters were appointed to teaching positions at government universities in the southern provinces. These five became known as "the Five Northern Tigers who went South." Besides Ku Ju-chang, this group included Wan Lai-sheng, Fu Chen-sung, Wang Hsao-chou and Li Hsien-wu. The Five Northern Tigers also were entrusted with creating a standard martial arts program that could be taught to the military and at universities throughout the country.

This proved to be an exciting era for Chinese martial arts. For the first time, masters of different styles from around the country were brought together to share knowledge and advance the fighting arts. Ku Ju-chang exchanged techniques with many different masters. Among the styles he studied were Hsing-I, Paqua and T'ai Chi (with Sun Lu T'ang); Wutang sword style (with Li Ching-lin); Choy Lay Fut (with Taam Saam); and Ch'a Fist.

After 1928, Ku Ju-chang spent most of his time in Kwangtung province, where he had many disciples. Among those disciples was Lung Tzu-hsiang, who had moved from Canton to Hong Kong around 1945. He found a position teaching Northern Shaolin at the Hong Kong Athletic Association, which at the time served as a center for many different styles of Chinese martial arts. In 1949, a young boy named Lai Hung, who later gained fame as one of kung-fu's greatest full-contact fighters, enrolled as a student in master Lung's class. Years later, in the 1970s, Lai Hung immigrated to San Francisco, where he passed on the Northern Shaolin style to his American students. Northern Shaolin also made its way to the United States and to many other countries around the world under the guidance of other disciples of Ku Ju-chang, such as Yim Seung Mou (Fig. 2.5).

Fig. 2.5: The two-person sparring form as demonstrated by Ku's disciples Yim Seung Mou (left) and Lung Tzu-hsiang (right), circa 1930s.

Chapter 3
LAI HUNG

A more complete biography of
Lai Hung has been provided in
*The Secrets of Northern Shaolin
Kung Fu*[3], but it is worthwhile
to briefly review his accomplishments here.

Lai Hung was born in Hsin-
Hsing County, Kwangtung
province, in 1938 (Fig. 3.1). His
father was an avid practitioner
of the martial arts, and when
Lai Hung was about 8 years
old, he began to learn a style of
kung-fu known as Hung Tau
Fat Mei with a famous master
named Lee Nam. This martial
system was similar to one that
Lai Hung would later study in
detail, Choy Lay Fut.

Fig. 3.1: Lai Hung, around 1960.

In the period between 1937, when the Japanese invaded China,
and 1949, when the Chinese Communist forces under Mao Tzu-

3. Klingborg, Brian, *The Secrets of Northern Shaolin Kung Fu*, (Charles E. Tuttle
Publishing, 1988).

Fig. 3.2: Lung Tzu-hsiang.

tung wrested control of the country from the Nationalist forces under Chiang Kai-shek, China was in a constant state of war. The elder Lai eventually decided to move his family out of China, and in 1949, they relocated to Hong Kong.

At the time, the Hong Kong Chinese Athletic Association served as the unofficial headquarters for martial arts training in the island territory. A number of famous masters from China left the country during the turmoil of the 1940s, with most eventually gravitating to the Association where they taught their systems and occasionally shared students with one another. At the age of 12, Lai Hung became a student of Lung Tzu-hsiang (Fig. 3.2). Lai Hung was to study with Lung Tzu-hsiang for the next decade, learning the Northern Shaolin curriculum, as well as Ku Ju-chang's famous

iron palm and golden bell (iron body) techniques (Fig. 3.3).

When Lai Hung was 17, Li Ch'ou, a disciple of Taam Saam, the man who is credited as the founder of Bak Sing (Pei Hsing) Choy Lay Fut (Figs. 3.4 and 3.5), entered

Fig. 3.3: Lai Hung performing the Northern Shaolin broadsword form.

Fig. 3.4: Li Ch'ou.

Fig. 3.5: Taam Saam.

his life. Lai Hung soon became of disciple of Li Ch'ou. During the period when Ku Ju-chang was exchanging techniques and students with other masters in Canton, he had sent Lung Tzu-hsiang to study Choy Lay Fut with Taam Saam. Now, a generation later, Lai Hung was learning the same style from Taam Saam's disciple. It is because of this unusual turn of events that Lai Hung is a lineage holder in both the Northern Shaolin and Choy Lay Fut systems.

Lai Hung is perhaps best known for his success as a full-contact fighter. His first competition was the Hong Kong-Macao-Taiwan tournament held in 1957. At the time, the custom was for all the Hong Kong masters to cooperate in the selection of fighters who would represent Hong Kong. They each chose a few of their students as candidates. The students then fought one another and the winners were selected to go to the tournament. Lai Hung was

Fig. 3.6: Lai Hung demonstrating the two-person sparring form.

Fig. 3.7: Lai Hung with the broadsword.

one of the students selected in this manner. During this period, Lai Hung was the recipient of special training provided by a number of Hong Kong's best martial arts instructors.

Held in Taiwan, the tournament became legendary for its brutality. In those days, a variety of very dangerous techniques were allowed, such as elbow and knee strikes, and fighters wore only thin cotton gloves to protect their hands. Lai Hung beat the four opponents he faced. He instantly became famous at the young age of 19.

Over the next 12 years, Lai Hung fought full-contact matches all around Asia, including Singapore, Malaysia, Taiwan and Cambodia. The fight in Cambodia is especially interesting because it was one of the first times that traditional Chinese martial artists faced "Thai-boxing" style fighters. The kung-fu fighters fared poorly, but it should be noted that they fought under unfamiliar rules and faced professional kickboxers who trained and fought for a living, while the kung-fu fighters all had day jobs and trained in their free time.

The following is a translation of a newspaper article from the Hong Kong Chien News dated May 18, 1961 detailing the Cambodian event.

Lai Hung Talks About the Fight in Cambodia
Miscommunication leads the referee to declare him the loser
Lai Hung shook his head when queried by the referee if
he was seriously injured—the referee took this to mean
he wanted to quit, so the fight was halted

The seven amateur fighters from Hong Kong returned on the 15th. Their defeat was not unexpected as their motive for competing was simply to gain experience. Now they will analyze their performance so that the Chinese martial arts community can improve. Our reporter had a special interview with fighter Lai Hung yesterday. Mr. Lai talked about his experience fighting Bing Leung.

Mr. Lai teaches Chinese martial arts at the Kowloon Bus Employee's Association, as well as at his own school located at 191 Ching Shan Road. According to Mr. Lai, the Cambodian fighters were all fierce and fast in attack and knew how to use their advantage of ring experience. The kung fu fighters and Cambodian fighters each had their special techniques, but the Cambodian fighters definitely had superior physical conditioning.

According to Lai, the competition had been in the planning stages for a long time, but for a while it seemed that it was not going to happen, until suddenly a month ago a notice came from Cambodia informing the Hong Kong fighters that the competition was on. The Cambodian organizers of the event suggested the Hong Kong delegation travel to Cambodia on May 2nd. The trip was delayed due to visa procedures, so the competition was rescheduled. The fighters from Hong Kong finally boarded a Cathy Pacific flight at 5 P.M. on May 8, and landed about two hours later.

The Hong Kong and Cambodian delegations finally agreed to begin the competition on May 9. The Chinese population in Cambodia was very supportive of this event. They heartily supported the kung-fu fighters.

In the aftermath of the event, and in Lai's analysis of Cambodian boxing, he believes the Hong Kong fighters do not compare to the Cambodians. Although the Cambodians do not train in a traditional martial arts school manner, they are very well organized. Boxers go through a process of selection and training. They train with iron rods, iron plates, punching bags, and so on. They remain light on their feet, yet can deliver enormous kicking power. Their fingers, fists, elbows, knees and legs can subdue an opponent in one or two moves. Their legs, especially, can attack without warning. Their left-right kicking combination is like two knives chopping from either side.

Bing Leung is a brave, well-known Cambodian boxer

Lai Hung's opponent was Bing Leung, a famous Cambodian boxer. According to Lai, Bing Leung was brave and skillful. Lai said that if the event had been held in Hong Kong, the audience would not be able to watch because of the unbearable brutality of it.

Lai Hung and Bing Leung were scheduled to have five three-minute rounds (Fig. 3.8). Lai said his loss was really just a matter of a misunderstanding.

According to Lai, in the first round, the two fighters engaged in light contact, trying to feel each other out. Both spent the round testing the water, so to speak.

In the second round, the fighters began to discover each other's technique, so the contact became heavier. Bing

Leung started the offensive with a strong punch toward the side of Lai Hung's forehead. Lai sank into a horse stance and hooked Bing's arm with his left hand. As he hooked the arm, he blasted Bing with a right punch. This punch had all of Lai Hung's might, and Bing fell to the canvas immediately after the hit. But then he jumped right back up again. The second round ended shortly after this exchange.

Lai Hung fell into trap
His forehead started to bleed

After two minutes of rest, the third round started. Bing Leung came at Lai with a full offense. In this round, he switched to kicking. With just a slight body movement, he was already in the air with a left-right crescent kick. Lai avoided the

Fig. 3.8: Lai Hung before the fight in Cambodia.

attack and counterattacked with a Choy Lay Fut strike. This time, Leung fell to the ground and stayed there. He grasped his midsection, showing signs of great pain. Lai Hung felt remorseful for hitting such a vulnerable spot. He actually apologized to Leung. At this point, Leung attacked. One of his techniques cut Lai's forehead. Lai was furious and charged forward, striking Leung heavily. The round ended shortly thereafter.

Lai says, my kick was fast,
yet his was faster

As both fighters stepped into the center of the ring for the fourth round, the audience clapped wildly. Bing Leung attacked with a variety of techniques, catching Lai off guard (Fig. 3.9). Lai was overpowered and hit. However, he was not injured. He counterattacked as he had in previous rounds and

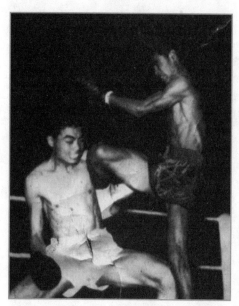

Fig. 3.9: Lai Hung on the defense against Bing Leung.

again knocked Leung to the canvas. As Leung got to his feet, Lai immediately attacked with a flying right kick. Leung was fast and locked up Lai's leg. He pushed Lai against the rope. The referee separated the two and paused to look at Lai's forehead. The referee, worried about Lai's injury, asked him if he wanted to continue the fight. Lai misunderstood and shook his head, trying to convey that the injury was not serious. The referee then stopped the fight. He did not announce a winner.

After the fight, Lai Hung told reporters, "It's only a competition. I don't care about winning or losing. Losing does not mean a loss of face. The trip was for experience. My only desire to win would have been to spread the art of kung-fu." He then praised the Cambodian fighters and said he admired their training methods and envied their frequent opportunities for fighting.

Lai Hung established his own martial arts school in Hong Kong in 1961. He taught Choy Lay Fut and Northern Shaolin and many champions emerged under his tutelage. In 1972, Lai Hung and his family moved to the United States, where he founded the Lai Hung Chinese Martial Arts Institute (LHCMI) on Columbus Street in San Francisco. He later relocated to Sacramento. Today, there are branches of the LHCMI in Richmond, Sacramento and Davis, Calif. Lai Hung continues to be recognized as one of the patriarchs of both the Ch'oy Lay Fut and Northern Shaolin systems (Figs. 3.10 and 3.11).

Fig. 3.10: Li Ch'ou seated (front, center) with his closest students. Lai Hung is seated to his left.

Fig. 3.11: A group photo of Hong Kong kung-fu masters. Lai Hung is in the second row, behind and to the left of the famous movie star Kwan Tak Hing.

Chapter 4
BASIC SKILLS

Traditional martial arts are guided by an ancient philosophy that has, in some sense, contributed to a decline in the integrity of those very ideals. In a Western society driven by the desire for fast results through minimal personal expenditure, many martial arts have been forced to reduce the emphasis on arduous and ostensibly useless foundational skills to attract and retain the next generation of students. For example, the practical minded (and, unfortunately, the lazy) may question the usefulness of long hours of stance training as it pertains to actual fighting prowess. In short, the very concept of kung-fu as "hard work" has come to be an endangered species of sorts in the modern era.

The intent of such training in the traditional martial arts can be viewed in two distinct ways. One major motive lies closer to fighting pragmatism than the other: to fight, the body must be properly conditioned. Cardiovascular fitness, flexibility, strength and stamina are all requisite for sustained physical engagements. Stance training, both stationary and dynamic, builds the deep-rooted lower body strength that translates to stability in movement. Extended postures and direct stretching of the body enables a maximum range of motion necessary to be a fully versatile fighter capable of striking at the safest distance and from multiple positions. The running exercises (e.g., knee strikes, punching while moving forward and backward, lateral cross-over steps) couple agility practice with pure cardiovascular training—a good fighter must be light-footed and not easily winded.

The other way of viewing basic skills training is one that really aligns itself with the "arts" in the term "martial arts": edification of character. In the same way that the underlying ideals of theater, dance, literature and painting are to explore human nature, action and ethical conduct (along with motives of an aesthetic nature), traditional martial arts seek to improve the person through his practice. The cultivation of the positive traits of humility, perseverance and élan are all deeply valued by the Chinese and indeed by most societies everywhere. Learning to fight concomitantly with learning to be a better person is said to be the most fundamental principle of the traditional martial arts.

Therefore, in the pursuit of becoming a complete martial artist, one must ply difficult, repetitive and often-boring basic training. Some fundamental skills that permeate all Northern Shaolin kung-fu (and in particular the two-person sparring form) are:

Basic Skill #1: "Square Horse" Stance

The square horse stance *(sei ping ma)* is similar to sitting on an invisible chair with the feet spread parallel to one other approximately twice a shoulder-width distance apart (Fig. 4.1). The weight of the body is equally distributed to both legs and feet. The posture of the upper body must be erect (Fig. 4.2).

This is the most fundamental stance in the Chinese martial arts, and many traditionalists refer to it as the foundation on which all other skills are built. Historically, all beginning students had to endure this stance for months and sometimes years before receiving any other martial arts instruction. It was as much a way of culling the diligent from the lazy as of strengthening the lower body.

Fig. 4.1

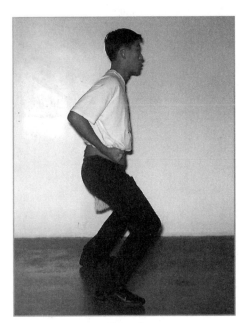

Fig. 4.2

Basic Skill #2: "Bow and Arrow" Stance

The bow and arrow stance *(chin gung hau jin)* features the front leg bent and the hind leg held straight. The front foot is angled inward and never pointed forward (Fig. 4.3). The weight of the body is roughly distributed to both legs equally; however, the weight distribution can be shifted slightly as required by the situation. With the rear leg functioning as a strut to support the body (Fig. 4.4), *chin gung hau jin* affords stability from front to back.

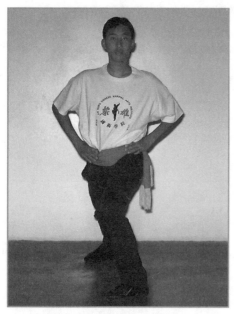

Fig. 4.3

Fig. 4.4

Basic Skill #3: "Rearing Horse" Stance

The rearing horse stance *(diu tai ma)* features a bent rear leg supporting the weight of the body. The front leg is also bent but hanging with the toes just touching the ground (Figs. 4.5 and 4.6). This horse is used for defensive maneuvering in a counterattack. As the body weight is shifted to one leg, the other leg is freed up for attack or for transition into another stance.

Fig. 4.5   *Fig. 4.6*

Basic Skill #4: "Horizontal Fist"

The horizontal fist *(ping kyun)* is held with the first knuckles level (Fig. 4.7). The striking surface of this fist is flat with the knuckles in a straight line. *Ping kyun* has two striking positions. One target position is when the punch is at the shoulder height of an opponent. The other target position is the midsection (Fig. 4.8).

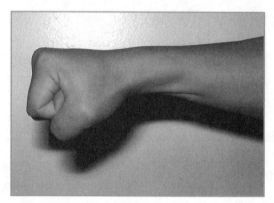

Fig. 4.7

Fig. 4.8

Basic Skill #5: "Vertical Fist"

The vertical fist *(yat ji kyun)* is held with the first knuckles vertical (Fig. 4.9). This fist is typically delivered at the shoulder level of the opponent (Fig. 4.10). This strike commonly occurs in the Northern Shaolin forms.

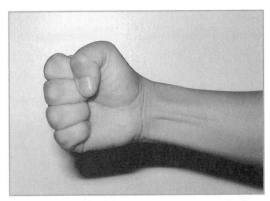

Fig. 4.9

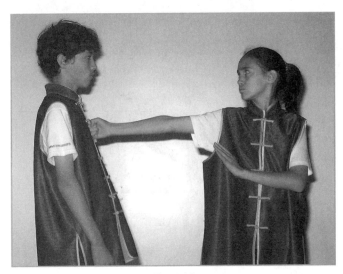

Fig. 4.10

Basic Skill #6: "Heel Kick"

This kick *(dang)* is delivered with the heel as the striking surface. The thrust of the kick is linear and directed toward the front. *Dang* is delivered in two smoothly linked steps (Figs. 4.11 and 4.12). The kick is initiated with a slight lifting of the thigh. The lower leg then extends and snaps outward in a straight, forward thrust. The heel kick is a penetrating frontal attack.

Fig. 4.11

Fig. 4.12

Basic Skill #7: "Inside Crescent Kick"
This circular kick (kam min teui) arcs toward the centerline of the
body and is the inverse of the outside crescent kick (baai lin teui).
In practice, extend one arm to provide a target (Fig. 4.13) and kick
the hand with the instep of the opposite foot (Fig. 4.14).

Fig. 4.13

Fig. 4.14

Basic Skill #8: "Sweeping Kick"

This kick is used to topple the opponent by upsetting his footing. The kick starts by lowering the body as one draws a circle with the kicking leg, simultaneously pivoting on the other leg. The compact sweeping motion uproots the opponent's stance (Figs. 4.15 and 4.16).

Fig. 4.15

Fig. 4.16

These basics skills are the principal building blocks of *deui chaak*. The importance of these simple elements from a traditional standpoint cannot be overstated. Some traditional masters judge the overall quality of a martial arts practitioner by the strength of his basic skills. Further (and especially in the past), many masters would confine their curriculum to these fundamentals for many of their students. Once competence has been achieved in these skills, one can begin to learn martial forms.

Chapter 5

THE NORTHERN SHAOLIN TWO-PERSON SPARRING FORM
(BUK SIU LAM YI YAN DEUI CHAAK)

Instructions for the Northern Shaolin sparring form are enumerated below, with the applications of the movements included in the following chapter. Special precautions must be taken with two-person forms, because they are essentially staged combat sequences. Since most of the movements are potentially injurious, practitioners should pay very close attention to their execution. If either participant moves too quickly for the other to react properly, an accidental strike or a hyperextended joint is possible. To help minimize this danger, refrain from using power in the various techniques until fluency with the form is achieved.

The sparring set is characterized by symmetry in movement: each person will perform many of the same moves in the same sequence but at different times in the form. One key difference lies in a particular move: *one person will flip the other.* Thus, we denote the "flipper" as Person A and the "flipee" as Person B. All directions will be given relative to the perspective of the individual in question, whatever his actual overall position may be. Whenever appropriate, the positions of each person will be given relative to the "stage front" (i.e., the initial point-of-view of the participants in the set) and the "stage rear" (i.e., directly opposite to "stage front").

1. To begin the form, both partners start in the ready position next to one other, facing the same direction (Fig. 5.1). Person B stands on the left side of A.

Fig. 5.1

2.   A and B: Bow at the waist (Fig. 5.2).

Fig. 5.2

3.   B: Use double push hands to push person A away while dashing diagonally toward "stage front" approximately two strides to the left, simultaneously turning the body 180 degrees to come to rest in the ready position, facing toward "stage rear."

A: Use double push hands to push person B away while dashing diagonally backward toward "stage rear" approximately two strides to the right, to come to rest in the ready position facing toward "stage front" (Figs. 5.3 and 5.4).

Fig. 5.3

Fig. 5.4

Persons A and B should thus come to occupy the opposing corners of an imaginary square.

4.   A and B: Bow again at the waist (Fig. 5.5).

Fig. 5.5

5.   A and B: Perform *bei lai* (Figs. 5.6 and 5.7).

Fig. 5.6

Fig. 5.7

6. A and B: From *bei lai*, open both hands and rotate them inward until their backs are touching. Keeping the hands together, drop them in an arc to the abdomen and then draw them up along the body to chest height, straightening the knees at the same time (Fig. 5.8).

Fig. 5.8

7. A and B: Without pausing, allow the hands to continue their arcing motion out and away from the chest and then downward below waist level; as the arms fall, allow the legs to bend slightly. Once below waist level, the hands should separate and begin to move away from the centerline of the body; as the arms reach full extension, the backs of each hand should brush past the thighs and begin to move toward the rear of the body (Fig. 5.9).

Fig. 5.9

8. A and B: Swing the still-straightened arms slightly backward and then upward while slowly rising up from the bent-knee posture. The arms should move together in a "windmill" fashion at the shoulder joint, as in a butterfly stroke in swimming (Fig. 5.10).

Fig. 5.10

9. A and B: Allow the arms to continue rising until they are at full extension above the head.

10. A and B: Press both hands down to the sides until both arms are straight and each hand is palm down and horizontal. Each arm should be angled slightly away from the plane of the body (Fig. 5.11).

Fig. 5.11

11. A and B: Keeping the posture upright, raise the right leg until the thigh is horizontal (Fig. 5.12).

Fig. 5.12

12. A and B: Perform a double jumping kick *(seung fei teui)* (Fig. 5.13). During the kick, cross the arms across the chest and then swing them outward to block an oncoming punch or kick.

Fig. 5.13

13. A and B: Land in a left cat stance *(diu tai ma)*. The arms should resume their positions just prior to the kick (Fig. 5.14).

Fig. 5.14

14. A and B: Leading with the fingertips, direct the hands in a circular motion parallel to the floor—first out and away from the centerline of the body, then back and around, finally circling inward toward the waist so they come to rest against the hips with the palms directed upward and the fingers directed ahead (Fig. 5.15). This is identical to the ready position *(pou kyun),* but with open palms *(jeung).*

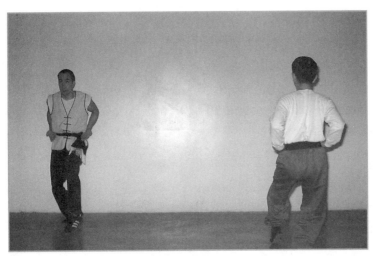

Fig. 5.15

15. A and B: Perform a crossed-arm overhead block: thrust the hands up diagonally across the body, coming to rest with the wrists crossed and touching above the forehead (Fig. 5.16). The point of crossing of the arms should rest about one-half foot in front of the face and held just high enough to permit a clear view ahead beneath the arms.

Fig. 5.16

16. A and B: Pronate (i.e., rotate inward) each forearm and form a crane beak *(hok jeui)* with each hand; the fingers should be pointing forward.

17. A and B: With the hands in *hok jeui,* swing the arms down to the sides so they come to rest angled down and backward (Fig. 5.17).

Fig. 5.17

18. A and B: With the arms in their positions in Step 17, retract the left foot slightly and then slide 45 degrees to the left into a left bow and arrow horse stance *(chin gung hau jin)* (Fig. 5.18).

Fig. 5.18

Both A and B should now be angled in from the opposing corners of the imaginary square, facing one another. The gaze should be directed at the opponent.

19. A and B: While keeping the knees bent, slide the right (rear) foot along the same diagonal as in Step 18 to meet the left (front) foot. Without stopping, continue sliding the right foot 45 degrees to the right to form a right *chin gung hau jin.*

20. A and B: Mirroring the previous movement, slide the left (rear) foot next to the right (front) and stand upright. While coming to a standing position, bring both arms up until they are horizontal, striking an imaginary opponent beneath the chin with the backs of both wrists. Each hand should still be tucked into *hok jeui,* with the arms straightened (Fig. 5.19).

Fig. 5.19

A and B should now be on a line parallel to the "stage front" and roughly bisecting the original imaginary square. *All subsequent movements will occur on this line until Step 96 near the conclusion of the set.*

21. A and B: In a manner similar to Step 7, bring the arms down in arcing paths away from one another toward waist level. Each hand (still in *hok jeui*) should brush past the thighs and begin to move toward the rear of the body.

22. A and B: Swing the hands out to either side, bringing them upward and then whipping them inward for a double fisted strike *(seung fung gun yi)* to the ears of an imaginary opponent (Fig. 5.20). The arms should roughly form a horizontal circle.

Fig. 5.20

23. A and B: Execute a double hammerfist strike: strike two imaginary opponents at an arm's reach behind you (Fig. 5.21). The arms should come to rest at full extension pointing directly left and right, with horizontal fists *(ping kyun)*.

Fig. 5.21

24. A and B: Swing both arms downward until both forearms cross a few inches above the wrist, with right arm over left (Fig. 5.22).

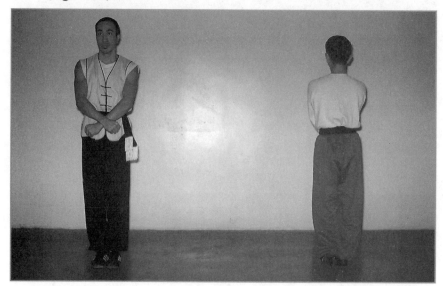

Fig. 5.22

25. A and B (Figs. 5.23 and 5.24):

    a. Right arm: Without pausing, continue swinging the right arm in an expansive, clockwise arc. The right fist will swing up and around more than 360 degrees until it comes to rest in front of the abdomen.

    b. Left arm: From Step 24, the left fist reverses its direction to follow in a clockwise motion slightly lagging the right fist until it comes to a rest in an open hand block at the right shoulder; the left fist will move through a smaller arc: roughly 270 degrees. The respective movements of the right and left arms take place simultaneously so that the left hand stops at the right shoulder at the same time the right hand arrives at the abdomen.

Fig. 5.23

Fig. 5.24

In the overall movement, the arms should appear to spiral out and then back in, with arms ending up crossed at chest height. The fists will be coordinated such that they will always be at roughly opposite points on a circle.

26. A and B: Draw the right fist across the chest and deliver a punch with a vertical fist *(yat ji kyun)* (Fig. 5.25). The left hand remains in its position in Step 25b, while the gaze is directed along the punching fist.

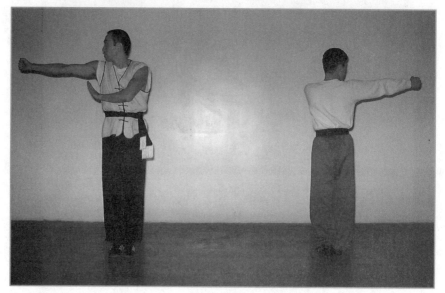

Fig. 5.25

27. A and B: Stomping the right foot, shift the body weight to the right leg as you settle into a right *diu tai ma*. At the same time, move the right fist into *pou kyun* and place the left fist over the right (Fig. 5.26).

Fig. 5.26

28. A and B: The left arm swings out in a horizontal block to the left and then circles around to end in *pou kyun* at the left hip as the right fist simultaneously delivers *yat ji kyun* to the left. In executing this movement, both participants will end up in left *chin gung hau jin,* facing each other (Fig. 5.27).

Fig. 5.27

29. A and B (Fig. 5.28):

    a. Right arm: Swing the right forearm upward and forward from the elbow in a circular motion with open hand, continuing the arc downward until the right arm is at the side of the body.

    b. Left arm: From *pou kyun,* raise the left arm upward as the right arm falls. The left arm should come to full extension overhead at the same time the right arm reaches full extension at the side.

Fig. 5.28

As the arms move in opposite directions up and down, slide the right foot forward and assume a right *diu tai ma* stance.

30. A and B: Perform Step 29 again, but reverse the movements of each arm: the left arm will drop as the right arm rises (Fig. 5.29). The arm movements should be initiated from the final positions in Step 29. As the arms move in opposite directions up and down, slide the left foot forward and assume left *diu tai ma* stance.

Fig. 5.29

31. A and B: Striding toward one's partner, perform *seung fei teui*, slapping the kicking right foot with the right open palm (Fig. 5.30). A and B should kick at the same time and target roughly the same point: the partner's head.

Fig. 5.30

32. A and B: Land in a square horse stance *(sei ping ma)* oriented such that Person A faces the "stage rear" and Person B faces the "stage front." While settling into *sei ping ma*, execute a bent-arm block (fist held high, elbow pointing down) with the right arm, while simultaneously moving the left arm into *pou kyun* (Fig. 5.31).

Fig. 5.31

The previous movements are preparatory and somewhat ritualistic in flavor. Choreographed sparring occurs during the remainder of the set. A and B will engage one another and alternately attack and defend using various combative strategies.

33 B: Strike at the midsection of Person A with left *ping kyun*. Transition into right *chin gung hau jin* while punching (Fig. 5.32).

   A: Drop the right hand and block the incoming punch with the forearm. While blocking, shift your weight backward to withdraw the body from the punch (Fig. 5.32).

Fig. 5.32

Fig. 5.33

34. Repeat Step 33, but reverse the roles of A and B: Person A will attack with left *ping kyun* while Person B defends (Fig. 5.33).

35. B: Deliver an uppercut punch with the right fist while withdrawing the left fist into *pou kyun.* Transition into right *sei ping ma* while punching (Fig. 5.34).

A: Block the uppercut by swinging the right hand upward with fingers curled in, intercepting the strike with the heel of the hand and making contact against the forearm of Person B. Withdraw the left hand into *pou kyun* and transition into *sei ping ma* (Fig. 5.34).

Fig. 5.34

36. B: Strike again at the midsection of Person A with right *ping kyun* while keeping the left fist in pou kyun (Fig. 5.35).

    A: From the final position of Step 35, swing the right arm down and across to intercept right *ping kyun.* Other than the movement of the right arm, the position of the body should be identical to Step 35 (Fig. 5.35).

Fig. 5.35

37. A: Quickly drop down and, with the weight shifted to the right foot and body balanced on the hands, execute a reverse sweep *(hau sou)* with the left leg (Figs. 5.36 and 5.37).

B: Withdrawing both fists into *pou kyun,* perform a retreating shuffle step, with right foot crossing over the left foot. Transition into *sei ping ma.* The arms may also be held out to the sides during this movement (as shown here) (Figs. 5.36 and 5.37).

Fig. 5.36

Fig. 5.37

38. A: Immediately after the sweep, stand up into right *chin gung hau jin* while withdrawing both fists into *pou kyun* (Fig. 5.38). Take a step toward Person B and execute a right heel kick *(dang)* at the midsection (Fig. 5.39).

B: Shift from *sei ping ma* to right *chin gung hau jin* to face
Person A and, at the same time, swing the left hand across to
the right to block right *dang* (Figs. 5.37–5.39). The right arm
should be straight but held loosely at the side in preparation
for the next attack.

Fig. 5.38

Fig. 5.39

39. A: Keeping the fists in *pou kyun,* retract the right *dang* and, planting the right foot firmly on the ground, step forward and execute left *dang* at the midsection of Person B (Fig. 5.40).

    B: Retreat into left *chin gung hau jin* by sliding the right foot back. Simultaneously swing the right hand across to the left to block left *dang* (Fig. 5.40). The left arm should be straight but held loosely at the side in preparation for the next move.

Fig. 5.40

Steps 40 through 42 are similar to the "advance/retreat" version of the "three stars" *(saam sing)* conditioning exercise. Person A will initiate a string of three hits, advancing toward a retreating Person B. The stances of each participant remain parallel to one another throughout these steps.

40 B: Perform a bent-arm block (fist held high, elbow pointing down) with the right arm, while simultaneously allowing the left arm to swing behind the body. Retreat into left *chin*

gung hau jin facing toward the "stage front" while blocking, moving on a slight diagonal away from Person A (Fig. 5.41).

A: After executing left *dang,* perform a bent-arm block (fist held high, elbow pointed down) with the right arm, while simultaneously allowing the left arm to swing behind the body. Simultaneously slide into left *chin gung hau jin* facing toward the "stage rear" by advancing slightly with the left leg, so that the stance is on a slight diagonal and parallel to the stance of Person B (Fig. 5.41).

Fig. 5.41

41.   A and B: Repeat Step 40, but with the opposite limbs.

B: Retreat into a right *chin gung hau jin* on a slight diagonal toward the "stage rear," while simultaneously performing a bent-arm block with the left arm, allowing the right arm to swing behind the body (Fig. 5.42).

A: Advance on a slight diagonal with the right leg to assume a right *chin gung hau jin* facing toward the "stage front," simultaneously performing a bent-arm block with the left arm and allowing the right arm to swing behind the body (Fig. 5.42).

Fig. 5.42

42. B: From the right *chin gung hau jin* of Step 41, execute a clockwise "windmill" block downward with the left arm (Fig. 5.43).

    A: From the right *chin gung hau jin* of Step 41, execute a clockwise "windmill" block downward with the left arm (Fig. 5.43).

Fig. 5.43

Now, Person B will shift to the identical kicking attack used by Person A in Steps 38 and 39, initiating this sequence instead with a left heel kick.

43. B: From the right *chin gung hau jin* of Step 42, withdraw both fists into *pou kyun* and execute a left heel kick *(dang)* at the midsection of Person A (Fig. 5.44).

    A: From the right *chin gung hau jin* of Step 43, retreat into left *chin gung hau jin* by sliding the right leg back. Simultaneously swing the right hand across to the left to block left *dang.* The left arm should be straight but held loosely at the side in preparation for the next attack (Fig. 5.44).

Fig. 5.44

44. B: Keeping fists in *pou kyun,* retract the left *dang* and, planting the left foot firmly on the ground, step forward and execute right *dang* at the midsection of Person A (Fig. 5.45).

   A: Retreat into right *chin gung hau jin* by sliding the left foot back. Simultaneously swing the left hand across to the right to block right *dang.* The right arm should be straight but held loosely at the side in preparation for the next attack (Fig. 5.45).

Fig. 5.45

45. B: Perform *seung fei teui* at the midsection of Person A (Fig. 5.46).

    A: Avoid the oncoming kick by performing a retreating shuffle step, with the right foot crossing over the left foot. While moving backward, swing the arms in an overhand motion: backward, then up and over the shoulders. Continue the swing in a downward arc and block the kick in a chopping motion with the right forearm. Come to rest in *sei ping ma* (Fig. 5.46).

Fig. 5.46

46. B: Right after the kick, land in right *chin gung hau jin* facing
Person A and strike with *seung fung gun yi* aimed at the opponent's ears (Fig. 5.47).

A: Shift your weight backward and lean away to avoid the
double punch. Intercept the hook punches by swinging both
arms inward from the sides: with hands open and palms
facing toward the body, sweep the upraised arms toward
the centerline of the body and block the *seung fung gun yi*
(Fig. 5.47).

Fig. 5.47

47. A: Pivot the arms inward and downward around the elbows
and over the arms of Person B. Once the arms are on top of
the opponent's, thrust the hands straight toward the hip of
Person B with double push hands. Slide forward into right
sei ping ma while pushing (Fig. 5.48).

B: Retreat into *sei ping ma* (Fig. 5.48).

Fig. 5.48

48. A: Perform *seung fei teui* at the midsection of Person B and land in *sei ping ma* (Figs. 5.49–5.51).

B: From the *sei ping ma* of Step 47, deflect the kick with the right arm while sliding past the opponent. Person A should pass to the rear during the shift in position (Figs. 5.51 and 5.52).

Fig. 5.49

Fig. 5.50

Fig. 5.51

Fig. 5.52

49. A and B: Perform a tornado kick *(seung fung teui)* in a left-turning direction (Fig. 5.53). This kicking movement rotates the body 450 degrees from the initial square horse stance. Land in left *diu tai ma* with the right hand over the left hand (Fig. 5.54). The palms should be touching just in front of the abdomen.

Fig. 5.53

Fig. 5.54

50. A and B: Turn the left hand over on top of the right hand.
Separate the hands by drawing the left hand down and out
in a clockwise direction while moving the right hand down
and out in a counterclockwise direction, allowing each hand
to brush the thighs as they move outward.

51. A and B: Continuing the motion of Step 50, form *hok jeui* with the left hand and sweep the left arm to a horizontal position. Move the right hand up such that the open palm stops just in front of the forehead (Fig. 5.55).

Fig. 5.55

52. A and B: Bring the hands together again, with the right hand over the left. Simultaneously shift the left foot a step to the left and assume right *diu tai ma*. The palms should be touching just in front of the abdomen.

53. A and B: Repeat Step 50.

54. A and B: Continuing the motion of Step 53, form a roughly C-shaped configuration with the left arm held aloft and the right arm bent upward toward the opponent (Fig. 5.56).

Fig. 5.56

Now, Steps 52 through 54 are repeated in a symmetrical fashion, with mirror image postures:

55. A and B: Repeat Step 52, but shift to the right to assume a left *diu tai ma*.

56. A and B: Repeat Step 53.

57. A and B: Repeat Step 54, but hold the right arm aloft with the left arm bent upward (Fig. 5.57).

Fig. 5.57

58. B: Stay in the left *diu tai ma* of Step 55 in anticipation of attack (Fig. 5.58).

   A: From left *diu tai ma*, stand up into a golden chicken stance *(gum gai duk laap)* on the right leg. Withdraw the right fist into *pou kyun*, placing the left hand above it (Fig. 5.58).

Fig. 5.58

59. A: With the arms in the same position as in Step 58, skip two
steps toward Person B. Once within contact distance, swing
the left arm out and follow it with an extended right *ping
kyun* into the body of the opponent. The left arm should
come to rest in *pou kyun.* Step into left *chin gung hau jin*
as the right punch is thrown (Fig. 5.59).

B: Retreat on a 45-degree diagonal with the left leg to assume
a right *chin gung hau jin* facing toward the "stage front,"
simultaneously blocking the oncoming punch with the left
arm. The right arm should be straight but held loosely at the
side in preparation for the next move (Fig. 5.59).

Fig. 5.59

60. A: Advance into right *chin gung hau jin* on a slight diagonal
toward the "stage rear." Withdraw the right hand into *pou
kyun* while delivering an extended left *ping kyun* into the body
of the opponent (Fig. 5.60).

B: Retreat on a 45-degree diagonal with the right leg to
assume left chin gung hau jin facing toward the "stage rear,"
simultaneously blocking the oncoming punch with the right

arm. The left arm should be straight but held loosely at the side in preparation for the next move (Fig. 5.60).

Fig. 5.60

61. A: Repeat Step 59, omitting the initial advancing steps (Fig. 5.61).

B: Repeat Step 59 (Fig. 5.61).

Fig. 5.61

62. A: Advance on a 45-degree diagonal with the right leg to assume right *chin gung hau jin* facing the "stage rear" while delivering a left uppercut. Withdraw the right hand into *pou kyun* (Fig. 5.62).

B: Retreat on a 45-degree diagonal with the right leg to assume left *chin gung hau jin* facing toward the "stage rear." Block the uppercut by swinging the right hand upward with fingers curled in, intercepting the uppercut with the heel of the hand striking against the forearm of Person A (see Step 35A). Withdraw the left hand into *pou kyun* (Fig. 5.62).

Fig. 5.62

63. A: Perform a forward sweep *(chin mo or chin sou)* with the right leg. Keep both arms upraised and close to the torso to shield the upper body (Fig. 5.63).

B: Perform a jumping outside-in crescent kick *(kam min teui)*. Jump up as the right leg clears the opponent's head and stop the momentum of the kick by slapping the right instep with the left hand (Fig. 5.63). Upon landing, assume left *chin gung hau jin.* Be aware of Person A crouched below.

Fig. 5.63

64. A: Without moving the feet from their final location in Step 63, rise into right *chin gung hau jin* and strike at Person B with closed right fist. Since the opponent is behind you, you must rotate slightly to strike to the rear (Fig. 5.64).

B: From the left *chin gung hau jin* in Step 61, use a counter-clockwise "windmill" block with the right arm to intercept the strike (Fig. 5.64).

Fig. 5.64

65. A: Again remaining in place, rotate to the left and assume left *chin gung hau jin,* striking at the opponent with a closed left fist. Turn fully to strike at Person B (Fig. 5.65).

    B: While shifting into right *chin gung hau jin,* use a clockwise "windmill" block with the left arm to intercept the strike (Fig. 5.65).

Fig. 5.65

66. A: Withdraw both fists into *pou kyun,* and execute a low left *dang* (Fig. 5.66).

    B: From the right *chin gung hau jin* of Step 63, use a clockwise "windmill" block with the left arm to intercept *dang* (Fig. 5.66).

Fig. 5.66

67. A: Retract the left leg quickly and, planting it firmly, rotate the body slightly to the right and deliver a low right *dang.* (Fig. 5.67).

B: Without moving the left foot, assume right *diu tai ma.* Use a "windmill" block with the right arm to intercept the strike, deflecting the kick behind you (Fig. 5.67).

Fig. 5.67

68. B: Surge forward and use double push hands to propel Person
A away, simultaneously transitioning into *sei ping ma* facing
toward the "stage rear" (Fig. 5.68).

A: Avoid the push by performing a retreating shuffle step,
with right foot crossing over the left foot (Fig. 5.68).
Transition into *sei ping ma* facing "stage front," withdrawing
fists into *pou kyun* (Fig. 5.69).

Fig. 5.68

Fig. 5.69

69. B: Withdraw the right fist to *pou kyun* and place the left hand above it. Initiate a lunging shuffle step with the left leg and, once within contact distance, swing the left arm out and follow it with an extended right *ping kyun* into the body of the opponent. The left arm should come to rest in *pou kyun*. Assume *sei ping ma* facing "stage rear" as the right punch is thrown (Fig. 5.70).

A: From the *sei ping ma* of Step 68, use a clockwise "windmill" block with the left arm to deflect the right *ping kyun*, simultaneously transitioning into right *chin gung hau jin* (Fig. 5.70).

Fig. 5.70

70. **B:** Assume left *chin gung hau jin* by sliding the left foot forward. Simultaneously deliver a left hook punch *(sou cheui)* at the opponent's head (Fig. 5.71).

    A: Retreat into a twisting horse stance *(nau ma)* by moving the right leg into position behind the left. Simultaneously swing the right arm up and out to block *sou cheui,* intercepting the blow with the forearm (Fig. 5.71).

Fig. 5.71

The most acrobatic sequence in the sparring set occurs next: Person A will throw Person B into a back flip.

71. A: Advance toward the opponent, sliding the right leg behind and below the left leg of Person B. Come to rest in *sei ping ma.* Reach around the opponent's abdomen with the right arm and place the left hand beneath their left thigh (Fig. 5.72).

    B: Assume *sei ping ma* and place the left arm horizontally behind the lower back of Person A and prepare to perform a back flip (Fig. 5.72).

Fig. 5.72

Person A is positioned behind and underneath Person B. The right arm of Person A will serve as a partial support and a reference axis of rotation for the back flip of Person B. Person A will also use the left hand to help propel the flip by lifting the left leg of the opponent, as well as provide a partial boost with the right leg from beneath.

72. B: Reaching up and backward with the arms, leap into a back flip (Fig. 5.73).

A: As described above, help propel Person B through the back flip while remaining in *sei ping ma* (Fig. 5.73).

Fig. 5.73

73. B: After landing, place Person A's right leg in a "scissor lock": put pressure on the knee by pressing the left forearm down above the joint and supporting the leg from beneath near the ankle, with the right arm (Fig. 5.74). The opposing pressure of the arms should lock out the knee. Standing upright with the leg, step backward in a clockwise half-circle (direction as determined from an overhead perspective) while turning with the opponent (Fig. 5.75).

A: Remain balanced on the left leg while being controlled by Person B (Figs. 5.74 and 5.75).

Fig. 5.74

Fig. 5.75

74. B: After turning through a half-circle, drag Person A a few steps along the imaginary line parallel to "stage front."

   A: Perform a "scissor-leg takedown": with the right leg still locked out, drop down on the left hand and place the left leg behind the opponent's knees. Grasping Person B's legs with your own, apply torque and throw the opponent to the ground (Fig. 5.76).

Fig. 5.76

75. B: Follow the leg takedown to the ground in a controlled fall (Fig. 5.77).

   A: Follow through on the leg takedown, finishing in a sitting position (Fig. 5.77).

Fig. 5.77

76. B: Roll to the right and swing the left leg in the same direction to pull it free of the "leg scissor." Continue this motion in an expansive counterclockwise arc through the hip joint and, when the leg begins to circle toward the left, swing the right leg free of the "leg scissor" and through an expansive counterclockwise arc as well. The momentum of the legs should be sufficient to allow you to surge to your feet, right foot touching down after the left foot (Figs. 5.78 and 5.79).

    A: While Person B pulls his legs from between yours, attempt to stomp their hip with the right foot (Fig. 5.78). As the opponent swings himself to standing, rising up toward you, escape from being trampled by rolling out of the way (Fig. 5.79).

Fig. 5.78

Fig. 5.79

The maneuver performed by Person B in Step 76 (for example, seen performed by Keanu Reeves in the film, *The Matrix*), along with the flashy "kip up" popularized in martial arts movies, is a common way of recovering one's footing after falling or being thrown to the ground.

77. B: Assume a right *diu tai ma* and withdraw the right fist into *pou kyun,* with the left hand above it (Fig. 5.80).

A: After the backward roll, stand into right *diu tai ma* facing the opponent, with fists withdrawn into *pou kyun.* The arms may also be held as shown in preparation for the next step (Fig. 5.80).

Fig. 5.80

Steps 78 and 79 include a grappling maneuver in which Person A places Person B in an arm bar, as well as an escape from the limb controlling movement. This sequence will be essentially repeated in Steps 84 through 86, with the roles of attacker and defender reversed. This is an illustration of the symmetry of movement in this set.

78. B: With the arms in the same position as in Step 77, advance into *sei ping ma* by sliding the right foot forward. This should bring Person A into striking range. Once within contact distance, swing the left arm out and follow it with an extended right *ping kyun* into the opponent's body. The left arm should come to rest in *pou kyun* (Fig. 5.81).

A: Swing the right arm toward the "stage rear" to intercept the right *ping kyun* (Fig. 5.81). Continue in a clockwise circular motion and, sweeping the opponent's hand to about the head height, rotate the hand into a palms-up position and grab the wrist of Person B (Fig. 5.82). Twist the arm and continue the clockwise swing until the opponent has been turned about with his arm behind them. Lock out the elbow with pressure from the left hand and, controlling the opponent with the arm bar, take a step with the left foot and then transition into a right *chin gung hau jin*. Press into the back of the opponent's left knee with the right knee (Fig. 5.83).

Fig. 5.81

Fig. 5.82

Fig. 5.83

79. B: Follow the sweeping block of Person A into the arm bar. Allow the opponent to press you forward, taking one large step with the right leg into a low right *chin gung hau jin:* the body should be nearly horizontal while the right arm is captive in the arm bar (Fig. 5.83). Without moving the feet, pivot to face the opponent, assuming left *chin gung hau jin.* With the right arm still in the arm bar, use your free left hand to push up underneath Person A's chin (Fig. 5.84).

A: Use the left hand to bend the opponent's left hand and fingers backward, easing pressure on your chin. Apply additional pressure to the left hand of the opponent with the right hand, forcing his hand down and away from the chin (Fig. 5.85).

Fig. 5.84

Fig. 5.85

80. B: Break free of the wrist manipulation by swinging the right arm upward between the arms of the opponent, knocking their grip loose (Figs. 5.85 and 5.86). Follow with right *dang* (Fig. 5.87).

A: Release the opponent's left hand and retreat into right *chin gung hau jin* by sliding the left leg back. Block the right *dang* with the left hand, deflecting it to the right (Fig. 5.87).

Fig. 5.86

Fig. 5.87

81. B: Retract right *dang* and assume *sei ping ma* facing "stage front." Continue the attack by swinging the right arm in a sweeping backfist strike *(gwa cheui)* (Fig. 5.88). Transition into *sei ping ma* facing "stage rear," leading with the left foot. Simultaneously deliver a left *sou cheui* past the opponent (Fig. 5.89), reverse directions and continue with left *gwa cheui* (Fig. 5.90).

A: Retreat a step or two into *sei ping ma* facing "stage front." As the opponent delivers left *gwa cheui,* block the strike with an upraised left forearm (Fig. 5.90). Grab the left wrist of Person B with the left hand. Simultaneously place the right hand over the inside elbow of the opponent and apply a downward force (Fig. 5.91). Pulling with both arms, drag Person B a couple of steps.

Fig. 5.88

Fig. 5.89

Fig. 5.90

Fig. 5.91

82. B: Counterattack by transitioning into right *chin gung hau jin,* stepping forward with the right foot behind Person A. Grab the left ear of the opponent with your free right hand and twist (Fig. 5.92).

A: Execute an inside-out crescent kick *(baai lin teui)* with the left leg at the opponent.

Fig. 5.92

83. B: Intercept left *baai lin teui* with the right forearm (Fig. 5.93). Place the opponent's left leg in a "scissor lock" (see Step 73). Drag Person A a few steps.

Fig. 5.93

84. A: From the back, reach around the opponent's head with the left hand and grasp the chin. Grab his hair with the right hand and twist the opponent's head to the left toward his shoulder (Fig. 5.94).

B: Release the left leg of Person A and use the left hand to grab the opponent's right wrist. Then, follow the head twist by swinging the right arm of Person A up and about while turning to the left (Fig. 5.95).

Fig. 5.94

Fig. 5.95

85. B: Grasp the opponent's right wrist with the right hand, lock out the elbow with pressure from the left hand and, controlling the opponent with the arm bar, take a step with the left foot and then transition into a right *chin gung hau jin.* Press into the back of the opponent's left knee with the bent right knee (Fig. 5.96).

    A: Follow the movement of Person B into the arm bar. Allow the opponent to press you forward, taking a step or two into a low right *chin gung hau jin:* the body should be nearly horizontal while the right arm is captive in the arm bar (Fig. 5.96).

Fig. 5.96

86. A: Without moving the feet, pivot to face the opponent, assuming a left *chin gung hau jin.* With the right arm still in the arm bar, use your free left hand to push up underneath Person B's chin (Fig. 5.97).

    B: Use the left hand to bend the opponent's left hand and fingers backward, easing pressure on your chin. Apply additional pressure to the left hand of the opponent with the right hand, forcing his hand down and away from the chin (Fig. 5.98).

Fig. 5.97

Fig. 5.98

87. A: Break free of the wrist manipulation by swinging the right arm in an overhand "windmill" movement, hammering down on the opponent's arms to knock his grip loose (Fig. 5.99).

B: As Person A hammers downward, bend slightly backward and then forward, attacking by clapping the hands in at the temples of the opponent (Figs. 5.100 and 5.101).

Fig. 5.99

Fig. 5.100

Fig. 5.101

88. A: Follow the momentum of the overhand hammer strike into a kneeling position to avoid the attack to the temples (Fig. 5.100). After avoiding the hand-clapping strike, surge back up into left *chin gung hau jin* and deliver *seung fung gun yi* at the opponent's head (Figs. 5.101 and 5.102).

    B: With the hands still close together after the double hand attack, move the arms outward to intercept *seung fung gun yi,* blocking the double punches with the forearms (Fig. 5.102).

Fig. 5.102

89. B: Right after blocking *seung fung gun yi,* push the opponent's chin away with the left hand while pulling his hair with the right hand, twisting his head toward his right shoulder (Fig. 5.103).

    A: Thrusting the left elbow up between the opponent's arms, seize the left wrist and swing his left arm in the counterclockwise direction, allowing the head to untwist.

Fig. 5.103

90. A: Swing the left arm toward the "stage rear," sweeping the opponent's hand to about the head height before rotating the left hand into a palms-up position and grabbing the wrist of Person B. Twist the arm and continue the counterclockwise swing until the opponent has been turned about with his arm behind him. Lock out the elbow with pressure from the right hand and, controlling the opponent with the arm bar, take a step with the left foot and then transition into a right *chin gung hau jin* (Fig. 5.104). Press into the back of the opponent's left knee with the bent right knee.

B: Follow the movement of Person A into the arm bar. Allow the opponent to press you forward, taking a step or two into a low right *chin gung hau jin:* the body should be nearly horizontal while the left arm is captive in the arm bar (Fig. 5.104).

Fig. 5.104

91. B: From the left arm bar, seize the left wrist of Person A and pull him off balance. With an expansive counterclockwise swing, pivot about and place the opponent into a left arm bar (Fig. 5.105). Take a step or two and transition into right *chin gung hau jin* (Fig. 5.106).

A: Follow the movement of Person B into the arm bar (Fig. 5.105). Allow the opponent to press you forward, taking a step or two into a low right *chin gung hau jin:* the body should be nearly horizontal while the left arm is captive in the arm bar (Fig. 5.106).

Fig. 5.105

Fig. 5.106

92. A and B: Repeat Step 91, but switch roles. Person A becomes the attacker and Person B becomes the defender.

93. B: With the left arm captive in the arm bar, reach down with your free right hand and grab the right foot of Person A (Fig. 5.107). Straddling the right leg of the opponent, sit down into *sei ping ma* and force Person A down toward the ground (Fig. 5.108). Advance a few steps, dragging the opponent along.

    A: Release the left arm of Person B and counteract being dragged by sitting down on the ground, kicking your opponent away from behind with the left foot (Fig. 5.109).

Fig. 5.107

Fig. 5.108

Fig. 5.109

94. B: Roll forward away from the opponent's kick (Fig. 5.110).

A: Roll backward (Fig. 5.110).

Fig. 5.110

95. A and B: After rolling apart, stand up and perform a left-turning *seung fung teui,* landing facing each other in *sei ping ma* (Figs. 5.111 and 5.112). Withdraw the left hand into *pou kyun* with the right fist above it (Fig. 5.113). Then punch toward the opponent with the left fist while drawing the right fist up next to the right temple, simultaneously transitioning into right *chin gung hau jin* (Fig. 5.114).

Fig. 5.111

Fig. 5.112

Fig. 5.113

Fig. 5.114

With the combat sequences complete, the participants will now step off the imaginary line parallel to the "stage front" and return to the opposing corners of the imaginary square described in Step 3.

96. A and B: From the right *chin gung hau jin* of Step 95, extend both arms forward, palms down. Take a large step diagonally backward with the right foot, returning to the diagonal corners of the imaginary square.

   A repeat of Steps 6 through 10 will occur to conclude the set.

97. A and B: Slide the left foot diagonally backward next to the right foot and stand upright. Simultaneously pronate each forearm until the backs of the hands are touching. Keeping the hands together, drop them in an arc down to the abdomen and then draw them up along the body to chest height, straightening the knees at the same time (Fig. 5.115).

Fig. 5.115

98.   A and B: Repeat Step 7 (Fig. 5.116).

Fig. 5.116

99.   A and B: Repeat Step 8.

100. A and B: Repeat Step 9 (Fig. 5.117).

Fig. 5.117

101. A and B: Repeat Step 10 (Fig. 5.118).

Fig. 5.118

102. A and B: Perform *bei lai* (Figs. 5.119 and 5.120).

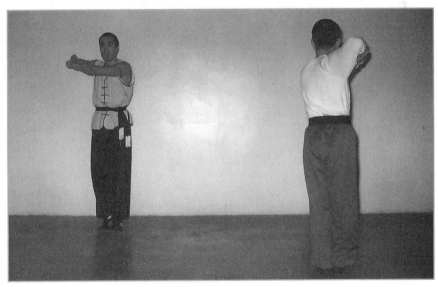

Fig. 5.119

Fig. 5.120

103. A and B: Bow at the waist (Fig. 5.121).

Fig. 5.121

104. A and B: Move quickly to the center of the imaginary square into the ready position, facing toward the "stage front" with Person B standing to the left of Person A (note that this is the original starting position of Step 1) (Fig. 5.122).

Fig. 5.122

105. A and B: Bow at the waist one final time to close the set.

Chapter 6
SPARRING FORM APPLICATIONS

Many diverse combat techniques are embedded in the *Buk Siu Lam Yi Yan Deui Chaak*. Upon viewing the sparring form, many of the applications are straightforward and obvious while others are subtler, and it is the latter that the traditionalist points to as comprising the "secret" portions of their martial art. This chapter serves to demystify some of these techniques (which have been both exaggerated and distorted in pop culture) by examining them in an objective way.

Before undertaking an analysis of the Northern Shaolin sparring form, one must become familiar with the specific steps of the set. Common sense indicates that one must "walk before he can run," so the reader must be patient in this learning process. It is the authors' assumption that most of the readers who reach this chapter and stage will have enough familiarity that detailed descriptions of movements in the applications are no longer necessary. Some difficult and/or important techniques will be discussed and explained in depth to aid the reader. It also bears reiterating that injury may occur if there is a lack of patience and attention on the part of either participant, so please use the utmost caution.

True understanding of the martial techniques contained in forms usually requires studying and practicing those techniques in isolation. One must focus on a useful movement or sequence of movements and explore them through repeated and dynamic practice. By working on a small subset of techniques in any given drill, one can refine and perfect his applications in an orderly and directed fashion. Also, these sets of techniques can be used in whatever order, speed and intensity that the participants desire, thus allowing the practitioners to develop a natural fluency and instinct for the movements in a setting that more closely approximates actual combat conditions.

In studying the sparring form, many techniques can be extracted that can be used directly with little modification to the "real world."

Technique #1: "Opening the Door"

We see this sequence in Step 48, with Person A performing *fun sau* immediately followed by *seung fei teui*. Northern Shaolin techniques often involve creating opportunities and then exploiting them—in a sense, opening a door before walking through it. Here, the swinging of the arms backward and outward in *fun sau* sweep the opponent's arms out to the sides to leave the body exposed to the subsequent lunging kick (Figs. 6.1 and 6.2). In practice, the expansive range of movement that is the aesthetic of the sparring form must be condensed for the sake of efficiency. We can achieve this by making *fun sau* more compact and explosive. When Lai Hung executes this technique, his arms only travel about a foot and a half, yet the impact with the attacker's limb(s) is so powerful and crisp they are easily knocked aside.

Fig. 6.1

Fig. 6.2

Technique #2: "The Arm Bar"

Deui chaak contains some basic grappling techniques (collectively referred to as *kam na,* which literally means "seize and hold"). The arm bar is a defensive weapon that allows the defender to quickly turn an incoming strike into a means of forcing the opponent into submission by hyperextending the elbow joint.

In the form, one can apply the arm bar for both low and high attacks. In Step 78, Person A intercepts a low right punch with the right arm, twisting toward the opponent's centerline (here, clockwise). The base of the intercepting hand at the wrist catches and guides the attacking limb, while the other hand applies pressure to the opponent's elbow joint (Figs. 6.3–6.5).

Fig. 6.3

Fig. 6.4

Fig. 6.5

We note some relevant variations. A more forceful and destructive response using this maneuver involves striking the opponent's elbow rather than applying firm pressure, which can cause dislocation and severe injury. Owing to anatomical function, the attacking limb must always be twisted toward the opponent's centerline (*as they face you*), thus for a low left punch, the defender must use the left arm to execute the same technique (here, counterclockwise).

In Steps 89 and 90, Person A is seized around the head region (note: one can also imagine being choked from the front). Here, the defender chooses to grab the left arm. To turn the attacking limb toward the opponent's centerline, the defender must grasp with the left arm. The subsequent mechanics are then the same as for the low attack. The symmetrical response can be performed using the right hand, again twisting the attacking limb toward the centerline.

The high attack occurs more commonly in typical combat, with strikes directed at the face and upper torso. The arm bar is a natural followthrough to a block/deflection of a high linear strike. A high right cross punch is efficiently deflected with the right wrist by the defender, who can immediately seize the attacking limb and apply pressure or a strike to the elbow with the left hand (Figs. 6.6–6.8). As before, the symmetrical response to a high left strike utilizes the left arm to block and seize.

Fig. 6.6

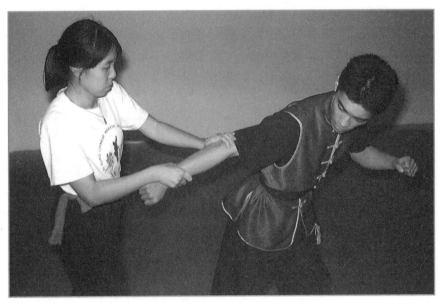

Fig. 6.7

Fig. 6.8

Deui chaak addresses both offense and defense. Once firmly applied, the arm bar is a good submission hold, because the subject is forced to bend forward away from the opponent. Defense against the arm bar requires a degree of anticipation. In the arm bar scenarios in the sparring form, the subject escapes in one of two ways. One technique involves relieving the elbow of the hyperextending pressure by counter-rotating the arm. In Step 79, Person B uses the rotation of his body to simultaneously interrupt the opponent's leverage and counter-rotate the arm to negate the arm bar. He can then use the free arm to attack the opponent.

In Steps 90 through 92, we see another excellent countertechnique to the arm bar. Person A uses his left hand to press his opponent into an arm bar. To escape, he pulls his opponent forward and off balance so he loses leverage, at which point he can easily counter-rotate the captured arm and escape. A natural followthrough here is to seize the opponent's formerly attacking arm and place it in an arm bar, applying the same technique as described above. The unbalancing of an opponent is a common strategy in Northern Shaolin and turns a defensive posture into an offensive posture to gain the upper hand.

Technique #3: Leg sweeps

If executed with speed and vigor, the leg sweep can readily topple an opponent and serve as an element of surprise. In the sparring form, the reverse sweep *(hau sou)* and forward sweep *(chin mo, also frequently referred to as chin sou)* are performed in Steps 37 and 63, respectively, by Person A. Rapidly dropping and twisting the torso helps maximize angular momentum and minimize telegraphy of the leg sweep. As a principal means of attack the leg sweep is ill advised; its efficacy is probably greatest when the opponent has been staggered or confused by some other method of attack. This is a high-commitment technique; failure to execute it properly places the user on the ground and in a vulnerable position.

Defense against the leg sweep requires good reaction from the defender. In Step 37, Person B recognizes and hastily retreats from the advancing leg sweep. The forward leg sweep has similar mechanics to *hau sou* but does not involve turning the back toward the opponent at any point. As in the fundamental form *dyun da* (Northern Shaolin Set #6), *chin mo* and *hau sou* can be performed sequentially to topple a defender who is agile enough to avoid the forward sweep. The combination of the two movements is called *chin mo hau sou.*

With the above caveats on using the leg sweeps, two interesting applications present themselves in the sparring form in Step 63. A plausible situation patterned on this step would involve using the forward sweep to counterattack against a high roundhouse kick, ducking low to attack the pivot leg and upsetting the attacker's balance. In the event that the kicker has executed a high jumping kick that the opponent has mistakenly gone after with a front leg sweep, a countermove to *chin mou* presents itself. As in Step 63, where Person B performs a jumping *kam min teui,* upon landing the kicking leg can be thrust forcefully backward to catch the opponent's sweeping leg once it swings past. This not only topples the attacker, but also stretches the legs out to damage the tendons of the adductors (i.e., the groin) (Figs. 6.9 and 6.10). These are, however, specialized scenarios that one should use caution in exploring.

Fig. 6.9

Fig. 6.10

Technique #4: Pushing hands

"Pushing hand" *(teui jeung)* techniques are underrated. Striking with the closed fist has greater popularity than striking with the open palm, but the latter offers advantages over the former. Using fist techniques against hard targets requires a conditioning of the knuckles against blows to avoid damage. Striking with the heel of the palm spreads the force of impact across a broader, more well-padded area, thus reducing the chances of incurring injury. One can also control the application of power such that the open hand technique is truly "pushing hands"—a powerful shove can be just as effective as a strike, unbalancing an opponent and sending him sprawling. The following scenario is patterned on Step 47 (there, teui jeung occurs as a response to *seung fung gun yi).*

Participants A and B should face each other at arm's length (Fig. 6.11).

1. A: Deliver a hook punch with the lead hand at the head of the opponent (Fig. 6.12).

    B: Sway backward to avoid the punch, using the lead hand to intercept and smother the incident strike downward (Fig. 6.13).

2. B: Thrust both palms at the opponent's midsection while sliding toward them, assuming *sei ping ma* (Figs. 6.14 and 6.15).

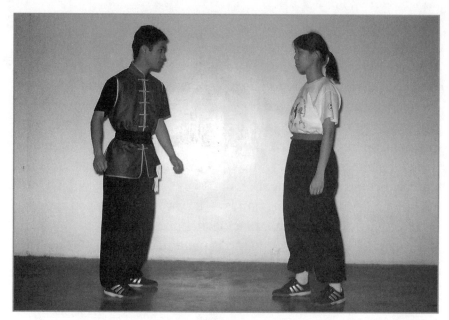

Fig. 6.11

Fig. 6.12

Fig. 6.13

Fig. 6.14

Fig. 6.15

The sides of the torso are vulnerable regions; ribs can be staved in to damage internal organs, for example. The application of force here (e.g, through *teui jeung*) is dangerous and one must take great care when practicing such techniques.

Technique #5: Takedowns

Forcefully taking the opponent to the ground is an effective technique in fighting; the very act of falling on a hard surface can incur injury. Such takedowns can even be deadly if the opponent is thrown in such a way that he sustains blows to the head and neck. Two instances of such techniques are illustrated in the sparring form.

The first is discussed in a scenario patterned on Step 74 and employs the "scissor-leg" takedown. Participants A and B should faced each other at arm's length:

1. B: Deliver a medium-height right heel kick at the opponent (Fig. 6.16).

    A: Sidestep the kick and catch it from below with the right arm. Put a "scissorlock" on the leg by pressing the left forearm above the knee cap (Fig. 6.17).

2. B: Plant the hands on the ground and kick the left leg forcefully into the backs of the opponent's knees, causing them to lose their balance and fall backward (Fig. 6.18). Complete the "scissor-leg takedown" by pressing the right leg into the opponent's body and use your body weight to wrench him to the ground (Fig. 6.19).

Fig. 6.16

Fig. 6.17

Fig. 6.18

Fig. 6.19

The "scissor-leg" takedown should be practiced with great care and preferably on a well-padded mat. Special attention should be paid to protecting the neck and the back of the head from impact.

The second takedown technique, illustrated in Step 71, differs from the one above in that the practitioner does not go the ground with the opponent. Agile usage of the square horse stance is the key factor here. With the participants facing one another at arm's length:

1. A: Strike at the opponent with a left punch (Fig. 6.20).

    B: Block the strike with the right hand (Fig. 6.21). Immediately guide the opponent's arm in a circular motion upward while sliding into *sei ping ma* behind him. Simultaneously thrust the right arm across the opponent's chest (Fig. 6.21).

2. B: With the right leg behind the opponent's left leg, push your thigh sharply forward while pulling the right arm force-

fully backward. The opponent should be toppled backward over the square horse stance (Fig. 6.22).

This technique should be approached with caution. In reviewing the five techniques discussed above, leg sweeps and takedowns require the most care. They inherently have smaller margins for error and require great speed and presence of mind to execute successfully. However, skilled kickboxers frequently use the leg-catching skill required to execute the "scissor-leg" takedown. Once the kicking leg is caught, the pivot leg can be kicked out from under the attacker without the defender having to go to the ground.

Fig. 6.20

Fig. 6.21

Fig. 6.22

Chapter 7
DRILLS

These techniques are difficult to isolate and practice, per se. They do not lend themselves to sustained and alternating drill work, with the possible exception of the arm bar technique. Two practitioners can alternately apply and escape from the arm bar, as in Steps 90 through 92. However, the chance of sustaining an injury is much higher than in other drills, because it does not take much force to hyperextend or otherwise injure the elbow joint.

However, two sequences from *deui chaak* can be nicely practiced in a continuous manner with great fluency. The first loops Steps 28 through 32 such that each participant takes turns initiating the attack:

Drill #1: Attack and defend in a fixed location.
With the same orientations as described in the sparring set text:

1. A and B: Stand in opposing square horse stances *(sei ping ma)* oriented such that the right foot of Person A is anti-parallel to the right foot of Person B (Fig. 7.1). While settling into *sei ping ma,* execute a bent-arm block (fist held high, elbow pointing down) with the right arm while simultaneously moving the left arm into *pou kyun.*

Fig. 7.1

2. B: Strike at the midsection of Person A with left *ping kyun*.
   Transition into right *chin gung hau jin* while punching
   (Fig. 7.2).

   A: Drop the right hand down and block the incoming punch
   with the forearm. While blocking, shift your weight backward
   to withdraw the body from the punch (Fig. 7.2).

Fig. 7.2

3. Repeat Step 2, but reverse the roles of A and B: Person A will attack with left *ping kyun* while Person B defends (Fig. 7.3).

Fig. 7.3

4. B: Execute *paau cheui* (uppercut punch) with the left fist while withdrawing the right fist into *pou kyun*. Transition into right *chin gung hau jin* while punching (Fig. 7.4).

   A: Block the uppercut by swinging the right hand upward with fingers curled in, intercepting the strike with the heel of the hand making contact against the forearm of Person B (Fig. 7.4). Withdraw the left hand into *pou kyun* and transition into *sei ping ma.*

Fig. 7.4

5.   B: Strike again at the midsection of Person A with right *ping kyun* while withdrawing the left fist into *pou kyun.* However, this time transition into *sei ping ma* (Fig. 7.5).

A: From the final position of Step 4, swing the right arm down and across to intercept right *ping kyun* (Fig. 7.5). Other than the movement of the right arm, the position of the body should be identical to Step 4.

Fig. 7.5

6.   Now, Persons A and B will switch roles:

A: Strike at the midsection of Person B with left *ping kyun.*
Transition into right *chin gung hau jin* while punching
(Fig. 7.6).

B: Drop the right hand down and block the incoming punch
with the forearm. While blocking, shift your weight backward
to withdraw the body from the punch (Fig. 7.6).

Fig. 7.6

7.   Repeat Step 6, but reverse the roles of A and B: Person B will
attack with left *ping kyun* while Person A defends (Fig. 7.7).

Fig. 7.7

8.   A: Deliver an uppercut punch with the left fist while with-
     drawing the right fist into *pou kyun*. Transition into right
     chin gung hau jin while punching (Fig. 7.8).

     B: Block the uppercut by swinging the right hand upward
     with the fingers curled in, intercepting the strike with the heel
     of the hand as it makes contact against the forearm of Person
     A. Withdraw the left hand into *pou kyun* and transition into
     sei ping ma (Fig. 7.8).

Fig. 7.8

9. A: Strike again at the midsection of Person B with right ping kyun while withdrawing the left fist into *pou kyun*. However, this time transition into *sei ping ma* (Fig. 7.9).

B: From the final position of Step 8, swing the right arm down and across to intercept right *ping kyun* (Fig. 7.9). Other than the movement of the right arm, the position of the body should be identical to Step 8.

Fig. 7.9

10. A and B: Repeat Steps 1 through 9 as many times as desired.

Drill #2: Attack and defend while advancing and retreating.
This drill loops Steps 58 through 62, allowing the participants to practice both the offensive and defensive sequences contained therein while practicing on fluid movement back and forth. This allows the practitioners to gain experience in coordinating hand techniques with mobility, which is a necessity in actual fighting.

With the same orientations as described in the sparring set text:

1. A and B: Stand two paces apart in left *diu tai ma,* with both arms held aloft (Fig. 7.10).

Fig. 7.10

2. B: Stay in the left *diu tai ma* of Step 1 in anticipation of attack.

   A: From left *diu tai ma,* stand up into a golden chicken stance *(gum gai duk laap)* on the right leg. Withdraw the right fist into *pou kyun,* placing the left hand above it (Fig. 7.11).

Fig. 7.11

3.   A: With the arms in the same position as in Step 2, skip two
     steps toward Person B (Fig. 7.12). Once within contact dis-
     tance, swing the left arm out and follow it with an extended
     right *ping kyun* into the body of the opponent (Fig. 7.13). The
     left arm should come to rest in *pou kyun*. Step into left *chin
     gung hau jin* as the right punch is thrown.

     B: Retreat on a 45-degree diagonal with the left leg to assume
     a right *chin gung hau jin* facing toward the "stage front,"
     simultaneously blocking the oncoming punch with the left
     arm (Fig. 7.13). The right arm should be straight but held
     loosely at the side in preparation for the next move.

Fig. 7.12

Fig. 7.13

4. A: Advance into right *chin gung hau jin* on a slight diagonal toward the "stage rear." Withdraw the right hand into pou kyun while delivering an extended left *ping kyun* into the opponent's body (Fig. 7.14).

B: Retreat on a 45-degree diagonal with the right leg to assume left *chin gung hau jin* facing toward the "stage rear," simultaneously blocking the oncoming punch with the right arm (Fig. 7.14). The left arm should be straight but held loosely at the side in preparation for the next move.

Fig. 7.14

5. A: Repeat Step 3, omitting the initial advancing steps (Fig. 7.15).

B: Repeat Step 3.

Fig. 7.15

6.   A: Advance on a 45-degree diagonal with the right leg to
     assume right *chin gung hau jin* facing the "stage rear," while
     delivering a left *paau cheui* (Fig. 7.16). Withdraw the right
     hand into *pou kyun.*

     B: Retreat on a 45-degree diagonal with the right leg to
     assume left *chin gung hau jin* facing toward the "stage rear."
     Block the uppercut by swinging the right hand upward with
     fingers curled in, intercepting the uppercut with the heel of
     the hand striking against the forearm of Person A (Fig. 7.16).
     Withdraw the left hand into *pou kyun.*

Fig. 7.16

7. Now Persons A and B will switch roles:

B: Advance into right *chin gung hau jin* on a slight diagonal toward the "stage front." Withdraw the right hand into *pou kyun* while delivering an extended left *ping kyun* into the body of the opponent (Fig. 7.17).

A: Retreat on a 45-degree diagonal with the right leg to assume left *chin gung hau jin* facing toward the "stage front," simultaneously blocking the oncoming punch with the right arm (Fig. 7.17). The left arm should be straight but held loosely at the side in preparation for the next move.

Fig. 7.17

8. B: Advance into left *chin gung hau jin* on a slight diagonal
    toward the "stage rear." Swing the left arm out and follow it
    with an extended right *ping kyun* into the opponent's body.
    The left arm should come to rest in *pou kyun* (Fig. 7.18).

    A: Retreat on a 45-degree diagonal with the left leg to
    assume a right *chin gung hau jin* facing toward the "stage
    rear," simultaneously blocking the oncoming punch with
    the left arm (Fig. 7.18). The right arm should be straight but
    held loosely at the side in preparation for the next move.

Fig. 7.18

9.   B and A: Repeat Step 7 (Fig. 7.19).

Fig. 7.19

10. B: Advance on a 45-degree diagonal with the left leg to assume left *chin gung hau jin* facing the "stage rear" while delivering a right *paau cheui* (Fig. 7.20). Withdraw the left hand into *pou kyun.*

    A: Retreat on a 45-degree diagonal with the left leg to assume right *chin gung hau jin* facing toward the "stage rear." Block the uppercut by swinging the left hand upward with fingers curled in, intercepting the uppercut with the heel of the hand striking against the forearm of Person B (Fig. 7.20). Withdraw the right hand into *pou kyun.*

Fig. 7.20

11. A and B: Repeat Steps 3 through 10 as many times as desired, with Person A omitting the initial advancing steps.

Drill #3: "Three-stars" conditioning.

This drill conditions the forearms and toughens them to absorb blows. Long-term training in *saam sing* (or "three stars") allows the practitioner to block and deflect strikes with great force, giving a defensive action offensive properties by simultaneously incurring damage on the attacking limb. The toughened forearms also can be used directly as offensive weapons. *Saam sing* is essentially included as Steps 40 through 42 in the sparring form. The drill can be performed in a fixed location or, as in *deui chaak*, with one participant advancing while the other retreats. A continuous, fluid drill is created by repeating Steps 40 through 42 so that, in addition to conditioning the forearms, the participants can practice using the waist and legs to generate power in striking, as well work on developing nimble footwork in both attack and defense.

The participants should be symmetric in posture as they face one another. Their movements must be synchronized so that the blocking arms meet along the common centerlines.

1. A: Advance into left *chin gung hau jin* while performing a low block with the right arm, moving on a slight diagonal toward Person B. The blocking arm should be held palm down while the left arm is allowed to swing loosely behind the body (Fig. 7.21).

    B: Movements are identical to A, but retreat into left *chin gung hau jin* by sliding the right foot backward.

Fig. 7.21

2. A: Perform a bent-arm block (fist held high, elbow pointing down) with the right arm by swinging the arm from its position at the end of Step 1 upward and outward in a clockwise arc (Fig. 7.22). The stance and left arm remain unchanged.

B: Movements are identical to A.

Fig. 7.22

3. A: Perform a low block with the right arm by swinging the arm from its position at the end of Step 2 downward and outward in a counterclockwise arc (Fig. 7.23). The stance and the left arm remain unchanged.

    B: Movements are identical to A.

Fig. 7.23

Now, Person A will continue to advance, repeating Steps 1 through 3 symmetrically.

4. A: Advance into right *chin gung hau jin* while performing a low block with the left arm, moving on a slight diagonal toward Person B. The blocking arm should be held palm down while the right arm is allowed to swing loosely behind the body (Fig. 7.24).

    B: Movements are identical to A, but retreat into right *chin gung hau jin* by sliding the left foot backward.

Fig. 7.24

5.   A: Perform a bent-arm block (fist held high, elbow pointing down) with the left arm by swinging the arm from its position at the end of Step 4 upward and outward in a counterclockwise arc (Fig. 7.25). The stance and the right arm remain unchanged.

     B: Movements are identical to A.

Fig. 7.25

6.   A: Perform a low block with the left arm by swinging the arm from its position at the end of Step 5 downward and outward in a clockwise arc (Fig. 7.26). The stance and the right arm remain unchanged.

B: Movements are identical to A.

Fig. 7.26

The sequence of Steps 1 through 6 can now be repeated as many times as desired. By reversing the roles of Persons A and B, the latter can become the attacker and the former the defender.

The above techniques and drills have been largely lifted directly out of the context of the sparring set. But there are other elements within *deui chaak* that can be assembled into constructive drills with the same focus and versatility as those above.

Functional fighting skill is a union of arm/hand technique, smooth footwork, and the usage of the entire body (especially the waist). Pragmatism demands that these aspects be efficient and adaptable to varied circumstances. Thus, they must be simple, direct and allow for some dynamic variation (e.g., the same defensive response can be used on a high attack whether it is directed to the face, neck or upper chest).

The following drills illustrate how elements of Northern Shaolin are incorporated and condensed into simple, yet effective fighting exercises.

Drill #4: Sweeping forearm parry versus jab/cross.
The sweeping forearm parry often appears in the Northern Shaolin curriculum. It is typically followed by a punch *(chung kyun)* in keeping with the opportunistic strategy of "opening the door" for subsequent attacks. In isolating this movement, we can begin by using it as it appears within the ten core *Buk Siu Lam* sets.

Participants A and B should face one another in square horse stance, *sei ping ma*, at arm's length from one another.

1.   A: Throw a high straight right punch at the opponent anywhere from head height down to the lower chest *(chung kyun)*. In the sets, the punch is formally executed from *pou kyun* (Fig. 7.27).

     B: Intercept the right punch with the left forearm, with the arm bent and hand held upward. Using the base of the intercepting hand at the wrist to catch guide the attacking limb, parry the blow aside (Fig. 7.27).

Fig. 7.27

2.   B: Throw a high straight right punch at the opponent anywhere from head height down to the lower chest *(chung
kyun).* In the sets, the punch is formally executed from *pou
kyun* (Fig. 7.28).

       A: Intercept the right punch with the left forearm, with the
arm bent and hand held upward. Parry the blow aside, using
the base of the intercepting hand at the wrist to catch and
guide the attacking limb.

Fig. 7.28

3. A and B: Repeat Steps 1 and 2 as desired.

Large, expansive motions characterize the movements of
Northern Shaolin and illustrate the principal aesthetic of the
forms. In particular, the sweeping forearm parry is performed with
an arcing sweep of the arm that ends with the arm held aloft over
the head to ostensibly afford protection from subsequent attack
(tiu sau). While this movement may be pleasing to the eye, its
practicality is questionable. Also, assuming sei ping ma to defend
against a frontal attack *(cho ma)* is foolhardy, since the stance has
no stability along that direction. All this serves to illustrate that
the traditional forms are not a blueprint for fighting but a means
of joining multiple techniques into a flowing and aesthetically
pleasing sequence.

We begin to see its utility when we take the sweeping
forearm parry out of this context and adapt it to a less-stylized

and more-mundane setting. We can repeat the above drill with two modifications:

A.   Replace *sei ping ma* with a more orthodox fighting posture: hands up and arm close to the head and body for protection; body and stance turned so that is nearly sideways. The body is oriented to minimize the opponent's target and the stance is more mobile in all directions.

B.   Dispense with the latter portions of the sweeping parry, concentrating on catching the incoming blow and deflecting it aside with a compact movement. Time the counterpunch with the parry to minimize the opponent's time to react (Figs. 7.29 and 7.30).

Fig. 7.29

171

Fig. 7.30

The sweeping parry is appropriate for use against high linear strikes. From the fighting posture described in A above, we can easily add another dimension to the drill by including hook punches. With hands up near the head, one defends a hook punch by simply pulling the forearms up and outward sharply (Figs. 7.31 and 7.32). The range of the hook is limited to within arm's reach: at the upper limit of that range, the hook is shallow and at the lower limit, the hook whips inward in a tight arc. The exact trajectory of the blocking motion depends on how tightly the incoming hook is delivered. A counterstrike can then be delivered by either the blocking hand or off hand. The same basic blocking motion can be used against the backfist strike, *kwa sau.*

Fig. 7.31

Fig. 7.32

By mixing the frequency and type of attacks (e.g., jab, cross, shallow hook, tight hook, backfist, high-low hook, attacking with either hand), we can create a practical and dynamic drill that contains the essence of Shaolin kung-fu.

While the sweeping parry is a technique for redirecting a high linear strike—say, using the left hand to deflect the blow aside to the left—we could instead choose to simply block the attack. The sweeping parry is necessarily a softer technique—a sharp blocking contact would knock the limb forcefully in the direction of the applied force, disallowing the ability to guide and deflect the blow in the opposite direction. The hard block is more direct and functionally simpler. With simple forearm blocks inward (to deal with straight punches to the head and upper torso) and outward (to deal with hook punches), one can provide basic protective coverage to the upper body. The following drill is similar to Drill #4 above, using compact forearm blocks in lieu of the sweeping forearm parry.

Drill #5: Forearm block vs. straight punch with counterpunch.
Participants A and B should face one another in the relaxed, orthodox fighting stance described in Drill #4 at arm's length from one another.

1. A: Throw a high straight right punch or jab at the opponent, anywhere from head height down to the lower chest (Fig. 7.33).

   B: Intercept the right punch with the right forearm, with the arm bent and elbow pointing downward (Fig. 7.33). Simultaneously rotate the right (front) leg by pushing the heel outward, causing the body to turn slightly behind the block. The motion should be quick and powerful yet subtle.

Fig. 7.33

2. A: Counterattack with a high straight left punch at the opponent anywhere from head height to the lower chest (Fig. 7.34).

    B: Intercept the left punch with the same right forearm, drawing the arm outward in a short motion to deflect the oncoming punch (Fig. 7.34). Simultaneously push the left heel outward, causing the body to turn slightly outward behind the block.

Fig. 7.34

3.   B: Without pause, throw a right jab at the opponent. The strike should be initiated from the upraised position at the end of the compact outward block in the previous step (Fig. 7.35).

Fig. 7.35

4.   A and B: Repeat Steps 1 and 2 as desired.

This drill illustrates the simple efficiency of the forearm block. In an orthodox fighting stance, the lead hand/arm can be used almost exclusively to block and deflect incoming blows. As the closest part of the body to the opponent, the lead arm can function as both the defensive and offensive "frontline" weapon: increasing efficiency by reducing both the time required for the user to respond to an attack as well as the time in which the opponent can adjust and counterattack. Having a strike follow on the "coattails" of a block is expedient and often unexpected.

Northern Shaolin (and northern kung-fu styles in general) is said to favor leg techniques over hand techniques. However, an examination of the sparring set shows a balance of these techniques and illustrates that a harmonious synergism of the two maximizes their usefulness. The next drill follows the pattern of Drill #5, incorporating kicking.

Drill #6: Forearm block vs. straight punch with counterkick.
Participants A and B should face one another in the relaxed fighting stance as described previously.

1.   A: Throw a high straight right punch or jab at the opponent, anywhere from head height to the lower chest (Fig. 7.36).

     B: Intercept the right punch with the right forearm, with the arm bent and elbow pointing downward (Fig. 7.36).

Fig. 7.36

2.   A: Counterattack with a high straight left punch at the
     opponent anywhere from head height to the lower chest
     (Fig. 7.37).

     B: Intercept the left punch with the right forearm (Fig. 7.37),
     simultaneously sliding the left leg backward. However, instead
     of assuming a right lead stance, immediately kick out with
     the left leg at the midsection of the opponent (Fig. 7.38).

Fig. 7.37

Fig. 7.38

3.   A and B: Repeat Steps 1 and 2 as desired.

In the above drill, Step 2B can be replaced with a low shin kick *(tek)* to the opponent's lead leg that closely follows the left forearm block—the angular momentum of the arm movement helps propel the ensuing kick (Fig. 7.39). Employing arm and leg techniques together multiplies one's chances of success in an obvious way: it is difficult to track and defend against simultaneous low and high lines of attack.

Fig. 7.39

The following drill also combines forearm blocks with kicks, in this case the "heel kick" *(dang)* and the "shin kick" *(tek).*

Drill #7: Sequential punching and kicking.

Participants A and B should face one another in relaxed fighting stances (see description in Drill #4). Person A will play the role of attacker and Person B the role of defender. The former will advance while delivering each strike, pressing the latter into a defensive retreat.

1. A: Execute *dang* with the lead foot to the opponent's upper body (Fig. 7.40).

    B: Perform a bent-arm block (fist held high, elbow pointing down), meeting the kick with a short, explosive movement directed toward the centerline of the body (Fig. 7.40).

Fig. 7.40

2. A: Execute *dang* with the rear foot to the upper body of the opponent (Fig. 7.41).

    B: Perform a bent-arm block (fist held high, elbow pointing down), meeting the kick with a short, explosive movement directed toward the centerline (Fig. 7.41).

Fig. 7.41

3.   A: Execute *tek* with the lead foot to the opponent's upper body (e.g., upper rib cage, upper arm) (Fig. 7.42).

B: Sidestep slightly to avoid the kick and absorb the remaining energy with the arms. With the arms in a fighting posture, the kick should obliquely cross the forearms and upper arms, distributing the impact across a maximal area (Fig. 7.42).

Fig. 7.42

4. A: Execute *tek* with the rear foot to the upper body of the opponent (e.g., upper rib cage, upper arm) (Fig. 7.43).

   B: Sidestep slightly to avoid the kick and absorb the remaining energy with the arms. With the arms in a fighting posture, the kick should obliquely cross the forearms and upper arms, distributing the impact across a maximal area (Fig. 7.43).

Fig. 7.43

5. A: Deliver a *ping kyun* with the lead hand at the upper body of the opponent (Fig. 7.44).

   B: Perform a bent-arm block (fist held high, elbow pointing down), meeting the punch with a short, explosive movement directed toward the centerline (Fig. 7.44).

Fig. 7.44

6.   A: Deliver *ping kyun* with the rear hand at the opponent's upper body (Fig. 7.45).

B: Perform a bent-arm block (fist held high, elbow pointing down), meeting the punch with a short, explosive movement directed toward the centerline (Fig. 7.45).

Fig. 7.45

7. A: Execute *sou cheui* with the lead hand at the opponent's upper body (Fig. 7.46).

    B: Perform a bent-arm block (fist held high, elbow pointing down), meeting the punch with a short, explosive movement directed upward and outward from the centerline (Fig. 7.46).

Fig. 7.46

8. A: Execute *sou cheui* with the rear hand at the opponent's upper body (Fig. 7.47).

    B: Perform a bent-arm block (fist held high, elbow pointing down), meeting the punch with a short, explosive movement directed upward and outward from the centerline (Fig. 7.47).

Fig. 7.47

9.   A and B: Repeat Steps 1 through 8 as desired. Switch roles
      so Person B plays the role of attacker while Person A now
      defends.

In reviewing the preceding drills and applications, one should
come away with a sense that truly practical fighting techniques
are uncomplicated and efficient. With these technically simple
skills, one can construct sequences of responses that are readily
adaptable to the changing nature of combat. Although this does
not dismiss the utility of more complex and physically challenging
strategies seen in Northern Shaolin and other kung-fu styles (e.g.,
using the tornado kick against an attacker to the rear, employing
a crescent kick against the knife hand of an aggressor, etc.),
it speaks to establishing a foundation of skills that are more
easily trained into instinctual response.

Appendix A
NOTABLE MASTERS

Listed below are notable masters, some of whom are in our direct lineage. Names are listed in three transliterations: Wade-Giles (Pinyin/Yale).

1. Chen Nien-po (Chen Nian Bo/Chan Nin Baak): One of the ten *modern* Tigers of Kwangtung (this term more commonly refers to the ten martial artists of the 19th century who were held to be the finest masters in the Kwangtung province. Arguably, the most famous of these is Wong Kai Ying, father of the Chinese folk hero Wong Fei Hung of the Hung Ga school).

2. Chiang An (Jiang An/Gong Ngon): One of the ten modern Tigers of Kwangtung.

3. Chou Shen-chih (Zhou Shen Zhi/Jau San Ji): One of the ten modern Tigers of Kwangtung.

4. Lai Kan-ching (Lai Gan Qing/Laai Gon Ching): One of the ten modern Tigers of Kwangtung.

5. Li Ch'ou (Li Qiu/Lei Chau): One of the ten modern Tigers of Kwangtung.

6. Liu Chin-tung (Liu Jin Dong/Lau Gam Dung): One of the ten modern Tigers of Kwangtung.

7. Lun Chih (Lun Zhi/Leun Ji): One of the ten modern Tigers of Kwangtung and a close disciple of Taam Saam.

8. Lung Tze-hsiang (Long Zi Xiang/Lung Ji Yeung): One of the ten modern Tigers of Kwangtung.

9. Ma En (Ma En/Ma Yan): One of the ten modern Tigers of Kwangtung.

10. Pan Chu (Pan Zhu/Pun Jyu): One of the ten modern Tigers of Kwangtung.

11. Fu Chen-sung (Fu Zhen Song/Fu Jan Sung): (1881–1962) One of the Five Tigers of Northern China, he was head instructor of the Nanking Central Guo Shu Institute. Founder of Fu style tai chi and an eminent master of *baat gwa*, he was famous for his fighting ability and his spear technique.

12. Ku Ju-chang (Gu Ru Zhang/Gu Yu Jeung): (1894–1952) One of the Five Tigers of Northern China.

13. Li Hsien-wu (Li Xian Wu/Lei Sin Ng): One of the Five Tigers of Northern China.

14. Wan Lai-sheng (Wan Lai Sheng/Maan Laai Seng): One of the Five Tigers of Northern China.

15. Wang Shao-chou (Wang Shao Zhao/Wong Siu Jau): One of the Five Tigers of Northern China.

16. Huo Yuan-Chia (Huo Yuan Jia/Fok Yun Gaap): Prominent master of "Lost Track Boxing" (Mi Zhong Quan/Mai Jung Kyun) and founder of the Jing Wu/Jing Mou Association in Shanghai.

17. Sun Lu T'ang (Sun Lu Tang/Syun Luk Tong): (1861–1932) Founder of Sun style tai chi and prominent master of tai chi, hsing-I/ying yi and paqua/baat gwa.

18. Li Ching-lin (Li Jing Lin/ Lei Ging Lam): (1884–1931) General of the Hebei-Shandong Army. Nicknamed "Magician of the Sword," he was considered to be one of the greatest Wudang swordsmen of his time.

19. Yen Shang-wu (Yan Shang Wu/Yim Seung Mou): A close disciple of Gu Yu Jeung.

Appendix B
GLOSSARY OF CHINESE TERMS

This is a collection of terms in common usage in our organization. In the practice of Chinese martial styles, a basic knowledge of terminology is important to gain a deeper comprehension of the spirit and intent of the art, as well as the practical aspects of having a common language for dialogue between master and student.

Many of the recent generations of Chinese martial arts masters, notably those who refer to their practices as "kung-fu," originated in the provinces of Southern China. Thus, most of the terminology of *kung-fu* reflects the Cantonese spoken language. Mandarin terminology typically characterizes those lineages that have more recently left Northern and Central China for the West. A key example is contemporary wushu, which has recently grown in popularity in the United States.

Before using this glossary, there are a few caveats of which the reader should be aware. Systematic study of the Chinese language by occidental academics has been largely confined to the 20th century. As a result, there is a preponderance of Chinese terms that were rendered in English before the development of self-consistent and phonetically accurate transliteration schemes. Most of these terms, which encompass geographical and proper names, persist in the literature. Some have undergone changes as a result of political pressures. For example, the replacement of *Peking* with *Beijing* as the name of the Chinese capital city in favor of the official spoken language of Mandarin in Communist China.

In addition, there was no standard transliteration scheme (or Romanization) that was used by immigration officials when the Chinese moved into the Western world. As such, any given Chinese surname may have been rendered multiple ways in English. To complicate matters, Chinese is a tonal language, so what may sound like the same name in English may perhaps correspond to different names/concepts in Chinese altogether: for example, the family name "Lee" may be one of several Chinese surnames.

Thus, the only true representation of Chinese is the written form of the language, which is independent of spoken dialect (be it Mandarin, Cantonese, etc.), as well as of any attempt at rendering the unique sounds of Chinese in any other language, which is sure to be imperfect. However, in academia, two Romanization schemes are preponderant and provide the most self-consistent and phonetically faithful ways of representing Chinese in English. The official dialect of the People's Republic of China is Mandarin, and the official Romanization scheme in use is Hanyu Pinyin (which replaces the older Wade-Giles system). Cantonese, the second most widely used dialect of Chinese and the most common language of kung-fu, is rendered in the Yale system.

In this glossary, we endeavor to rectify the inconsistency that exists in the literature concerning the Chinese martial arts. On the whole, we will use the Yale system of representing Cantonese, where we drop the tone number suffix. Certain terms, though less phonetically correct, are retained in deference to more established usage—in particular, geographical locations—since these are the renderings that are most readily recognizable. In addition, Pinyin Romanization is occasionally used in recognition of the preponderance of those specific terms (i.e., "Shaolin" rather than *"Siu Lam"*).

One should keep in mind that Chinese is a monosyllabic word language, that is, each symbol embodies a single concept (or set of concepts) and is represented vocally as a single sound. Thus, the imperfection inherent in attempting to represent Chinese sounds phonetically in English leads to pronunciations that may appear to have multiple syllables. Rather, these are an approximate representation of the diphthongs of the Chinese language as phoneticized in written English: for example, the surname "Louie" is typically pronounced "Loo-wee," when it actually is a single syllable that sounds like the Yale *Leui*.

The basic format of the glossary is as follows:

English Term: *Yale Cantonese transliteration* "Direct Translation of Characters"
Short Definition

Note: If a particular term has no common English description, the Yale Cantonese transliteration is used.

Backfist Strike: *Gwa Cheui* "Suspended Strike"
A circular strike delivered in a roughly horizontal plane toward the centerline of a target, leading with the back of the hand and striking with the knuckles; power is generated in this strike by rotation of the torso.

Baat Ji Geuk: "Eight Character Feet"
The splaying of the feet outward from the centerline when assuming *sei ping ma* (see **Square Horse Stance**). This positioning of the feet, viewed as poor form and a weakening of the integrity of the stance, takes its name from the resemblance to the character for the number "eight."

Bei Lai: "Give Courtesy"

The call to assume the formal bow of the kung-fu school. This show of respect accompanies the beginning of every set, and typically takes the form of a fist covered by an open hand combined with some form of stance. This has its origins in 18th-century China, when it served as a means of identifying people loyal to the revolutionaries hoping to overthrow the reigning Manchurian Qing government.

Bow and Arrow Stance: *Chin Gung Hau Jin* "Front Bow, Rear Arrow"

A stance in which one leg is bent to the front of the body while the other is held straight to the rear of the body. The bent front leg represents the curve of the bow (weapon), while the bracing rear leg represents the straight shaft of an arrow.

Cat Stance: *Diu Tai Ma* "Hanging Hoof Horse"

A stance in which, with the torso held erect, one leg is bent to the front of the body while the other supports the body from beneath. All of the body weight is borne on the rear supporting leg. Also referred to as a "rearing horse stance."

Chinese Martial Art Institute: *Gwok Seut Hok Yun* "National Art Institute"

A school providing instruction in traditional Chinese martial arts. "Gwok seut" (national art) is a common term used to refer to the Chinese martial arts, and is used interchangeably with "kung-fu."

Cho Ma: "Sit (in) Horse"

To assume the square horse stance, *sei ping ma*. Also the name of Set #3 in the Northern Shaolin curriculum.

Choy Lay Fut: *Choi Lei Fat*

A Southern Chinese martial art founded in 1836 by Chan Heung. As was tradition, the synthesis of Northern and Southern Shaolin disciplines into a unique style was named after the founder's three teachers: Choi Fuk, Lei Yau Saan and Chan Yun Wu. "Fut" is a contraction of "Fut-To," the Chinese phoneticization of "Buddha"; as all Chan Heung's teachers were trained in Shaolin kung-fu, he used "fut" to pay homage to Chan Buddhism ["Chan" refers to the meditative practices (Mandarin phoneticization of the Indian dhyana, meaning "contemplation") that characterize the branch of Buddhism practiced by the monks of Shaolin, known as "Zen" in Japan].

Chung Kyun: "Charging Fist"

The act of throwing a punch, with the implication that it is executed in an explosive manner. Also, the proper term for the so-called "one-inch" punch.

Crane Beak: *Hok Jeui* "Crane's Beak"

The formation of the hand in which, with the wrist bent inward, the fingers are held together such that their tips converge into a point. The configuration is supposed to resemble the beak of the crane.

Crescent Kick, Inside-Out: *Baai Lin Teui* "Swinging-Continuously Legs"

A circular kick delivered in a roughly vertical plane away from the midline of the target, striking with the outside edge of the foot.

Crescent Kick, Outside-In: *Gwa Min Teui* "Suspended-Facing Legs"

A circular kick delivered in a roughly vertical plane toward the midline of the target, striking with the instep of the foot.

Directions:
  Left Side *Jo Bin* "Left side"
  Right Side *Yau Bin* "Right side"
  Forward *Chin Bin* "Front side"
  Behind *Hau Bin* "Rear side"

Dit Da Gou: "Falling Hitting Ointment"
  A traditional Chinese medicine used to enhance the healing of superficial injuries incurred during the course of martial training. More commonly formulated in an ethyl alcohol base *(dit da jau* or "falling hitting wine")*.

Double Kick: *Seung Fei Teui* "Paired Flying Legs"
  A forward, leaping kick in which one leg generates forward and upward momentum while the other leg kicks out at the peak of the jump.

Fist: *Kyun* "Fist; Forms (of Combat)"
  This is the generic term for the various closed hand formations, but typically refers to the colloquial definition: fingers clenched with thumb bent and overlaid on the index and middle fingers.
  In other contexts, this term refers to the forms or sets of the Chinese martial arts, those choreographed collection of movements and postures that comprise the traditional curriculum of Asian combatives. It can sometimes, in a broader sense, refer to particular styles of Chinese martial arts.

Front Leg Sweep: *Chin Mo, Chin Sou* "Front Grind, Front Sweep"
  A swift leg sweep in which the shin is used to knock out the opponent's legs from under him. Can be used in conjunction with the rear leg sweep, *hau sou,* in which case the sequence is known as *chin mo hau sou* (e.g. in Northern Shaolin Set #6).

Fun Sau: "Separate Hands"

An outward block with both arms simultaneously traveling backward and away from the centerline.

Gaak Saam Sing: "Pattern Three Stars"

The conditioning of the forearms by the endurance of repeated blows. Usually performed with one or two partners, these blows are sustained from three "sides" of the forearm. A common practice in the kung-fu styles of Southern China, this conditioning traditionally requires the subsequent application of medicines to promote healing **(see *Dit Da Gou*).**

Gaau Jin Sau: "Scissor Hands"

A movement in which the palms are brought together in front of the body, swiveled on their heels such that the hands swap positions above and below one another. Utilized as a means of capturing an opponent's arm and placing them in an arm bar.

Gaau Jin Geuk: "Scissor Feet"

A movement used to recover one's footing after falling: the legs swing sequentially in a circle, and the resulting angular momentum is used to propel the body to standing.

Golden Chicken Stance: *Gam Gai Duk Laap* "Golden Chicken Single (Leg) Stance"

A stance in which, with the torso held erect, one leg is held bent and high, while the supporting leg is held straight through the knee. The spirit of the posture is that of a fowl poised for attack.

Hammer-Fist Strike: *Pek Cheui* "Splitting Strike"

A strike delivered with the inside of the wrist facing upward, hitting a target with the forearm or fist; power is generated in this strike by rotation of the torso. This strike can be used for both offensive and defensive purposes.

Heel Kick: *Dang* "Stepping (Kick)"
A front kick delivered with the heel of the foot against a target.

Hei Gung: "Air Work"
The practice of cultivating a synergy between breathing and coordination to enhance physical power in movement, the ability of the body to absorb blows, and in one's overall state of health.

Horizontal Fist: *Ping Kyun* "Level Fist"
A fist with knuckles held in a horizontal line, thumb facing toward the midline of the body.

Hung Tau Fat Mei: *Hung Tau Fat Mei*
A Southern style of kung-fu similar to Choy Lay Fut, characterized in practice by slow movements and low stances.

Hyun Sau: "Circling Hand"
A sweeping inward block with the wrist or forearm; the arm travels toward the centerline, intercepting a blow with the little finger side of the limb, before arcing down and away from the body. Used to block and parry blows.

Iron Palm: *Tit Sa Jeung* "Iron Sand Palm"
The practice of toughening the striking surfaces of the hand by progressively hitting harder and rougher materials. Traditionally, this involves thrusting the hands into increasingly coarse sand and rock, and striking grain or sand filled bags. The use of *dit da gou* **(see entry above)** during this training helps to prevent debilitating injury.

Kam Na: "Seize Hold"

The general term for jointlocks, limb manipulation and submission techniques. More commonly known by the Mandarin appellation "Chin Na/Qinna."

Kiu Sau: "Bridge Hand"

A general term that refers to arm techniques as utilized against an opponent; the bridging of the distance between a person and his opponent using the arms, both offensively and defensively.

Kung-Fu: *Gung Fu* "Hard Work"

A generic term for Chinese martial arts, usually for the hard "external" styles. The term connotes those positive results and benefits attained through hard work (the character "gung" is a combination of the characters for "work" and "strength"). Kung-fu is a descriptive term that is rarely used to describe martial arts in China, where the term *gwok seut (guo shu* in Pinyin) prevails (**see Chinese Martial Arts Institute**).

Lion Dance: *Mou Si* "Dance (of the) Lion"

The traditional ceremonial Chinese dance performed by pairs of people dressed in hand-crafted Chinese lion costumes; the dance is used in celebration and is believed to bring good luck by appeasing the gods and warding off evil spirits.

Lion Head: *Si Tau* "Lion Head"

The head of the ceremonial Chinese lion costume used in traditional lion dance; more loosely, the entire lion costume.

Mirror Hand: *Mei Yan Jiu Geng* "Beautiful Person Beholding Mirror"

An inward block with the wrist or forearm; the arm travels toward the centerline, intercepting a blow with the little finger side of the limb. The name refers to the resemblance of the movement to a person gazing into a handheld mirror.

Northern Shaolin: *Buk Siu Lam* "Northern Young Forest"
A Northern Chinese martial art with its origins in the Shaolin temple.

Numbers:
One: *Yat* "One"
Two: *Yi* "Two"
Three: *Saam* "Three"
Four: *Sei* "Four"
Five: *Ng* "Five"
Six: *Luk* "Six"
Seven: *Chat* "Seven"
Eight: *Baat* "Eight"
Nine: *Gau* "Nine"
Ten: *Sap* "Ten"

Opponent: *Deui Sau* "Opposing Hand"
One's opponent in either formalized or free-form combat.

Palm: *Jeung* "Palm (of Hand)"
The formation of the hand in which the hand is held flat, with the fingers held together.

Paau Cheui: "Cannon Strike"
An uppercut punch.

Pou Kyun: "Carrying Fists"
The posture in which the fists are held, knuckles facing downward, at the waist; the generic position of the arms from which punches are usually initiated.

Rear Leg Sweep: *Hau Sou* "Rear Sweep"
A swift leg sweep in which the heel or back of the leg is used to knock out the opponent's legs from under him (**see Front Leg Sweep**).

Roundhouse Punch: *Sou Cheui* "Sweeping Strike"
A circular punch delivered in a roughly horizontal plane toward the midline of a target, striking with the knuckles; power is generated in this punch by rotation of the torso.

Sabers, Double: *Seung Dou* "Paired Sabers"
A pair of sabers used together, with handles of semicircular cross-section, which allow a pair of such weapons to occupy a single scabbard, side by side.

Saber, Single: *Daan Dou* "Single Saber"
One of the four basic Chinese weapons: a slightly curved sword with a single cutting edge. Traditionally, the weapon of infantry.

Set (see Fist)

Seung Fung Gun Yi: "Paired Winds Pouring (Into The) Ears"
A fist strike performed by each arm simultaneously and directed at the ears or temple of an opponent.

Shin Kick: *Tek* "Kick"
A front kick delivered with the top of the foot or shin against a target.

Sidai: *Si Dai* "Younger Brother (of same) Teacher"
The Cantonese term used by a student for a male student who has joined their kung-fu school after them; a junior male student of the same generation.

Sifu: *Si Fu* "Teacher Father"

The Cantonese term for a teacher of the martial arts. Can be more loosely applied to any instructor of a physical discipline or skill.

Sigung: *Si Gung* "Teacher Grandfather"

The Cantonese term used by a student for the teacher of his sifu (commonly referred to in English as "grandmaster").

Sihing: *Si Hing* "Older Brother (of same) Teacher"

The Cantonese term used by a student for a male student who has joined the kung-fu school before them; a senior male student of the same generation.

Sije: *Si Je* "Older Sister (of same) Teacher"

The Cantonese term used by a student for a female student who has joined the kung-fu school before them; a senior female student of the same generation.

Sijou: *Si Jou* "Forefather (of same) Teacher"

The Cantonese term used by a student for the teacher of his sigung (commonly referred to in English as "great grandmaster"); loosely, any teacher in the student's lineage from generations preceding their sigung.

Simou: *Si Mou* "Teacher Mother"

The Cantonese term used by a student for the wife of their *sifu*.

Simui: *Si Mui* "Younger Sister (of same) Teacher"

The Cantonese term used by a student for a female student who has joined the kung-fu school after them; a junior female student of the same generation.

Single Straight Sword: *Daan Gim* "Single Sword"

One of the four basic Chinese weapons: a double-edged straight sword. Traditionally, a weapon used by officers and statesmen, as it is held to be more refined than the *dou* (**see Saber**).

Sparring: *Deui Chaak* "Opposing-Break Up"

A term used to denote various empty-hand and weapon sparring forms with two or more participants. By itself, it is an abbreviated way of referring to such forms. More properly used as "versus" (e.g., *daan dau deui chaak hung ying cheung* or single saber versus red cherry blossom spear).

Spear: *Hung Ying Cheung* "Red Cherry (Blossom) Spear"

One of the four basic Chinese weapons: a staff, roughly seven feet long, with a metal point mounted at one end. Commonly referred to as the "king of weapons" for its reach and killing potential, as well as the great skill required to wield it. The optional prefix *hung ying* refers to the red-dyed horse-hair tassel tied to the base of the spearhead, originally used to help absorb blood and prevent it from running onto the staff.

Square Horse Stance: *Sei Ping Ma* "Four Level Horse"

A stance in which, with the torso held erect, the legs are bent and angled away from the midline of the body. The knees are roughly positioned over the feet, with the thighs angled downward slightly below the horizontal plane. The configuration is supposed to resemble a person astride a horse. The term "sei" refers to the resemblance the stance has to the Chinese character for "four."

Staff: *Gwan* "Staff"

One of the four basic Chinese weapons: a staff of varying length, typically taller than the wielder.

Sweep Kick: *Liu* "Lifting-Up (Kick)"
A sweeping kick used to knock an opponent's feet out from under them, striking the target low with the lower shin or instep of the foot.

Teui Jeung: "Pushing Palms"
A thrusting push with both palms, usually performed while advancing sideways in *sei ping ma* (**see Square Horse Stance**).

Teui Mo Sau: "Pushing-Grinding Hands"
An exercise in which participants attempt to gain superiority over their opponent either offensively or defensively, while trying to maintain contact only through the hands and wrists. Is intended as an analysis in sensitivity and in the efficient usage of power.

Tiger Claw: *Fu Jaau* "Tiger Claw"
The formation of the hand in which the fingers are bent into a claw-like position. The configuration is supposed to resemble the seizing and rending paw of the tiger.

Tiu Sau: "Carrying Hand"
The upraised hand, held aloft to protect the head from blows from above.

Tornado Kick: *Syun Fung Teui* "Revolving Wind Legs"
A spinning kick delivered with instep of the foot against a target initially behind the kicker.

Twisting Horse Stance: *Nau Ma* "Twisting Horse"
A stance in which, with the torso held erect, the legs are bent and positioned against one another; one leg is placed to the front of the body with toes angled outward, while the other

leg is placed behind with knee braced against the front leg and trailing off to one side. The term refers to the twisting of the torso used to assume this stance in transition from the square horse stance.

Vertical Fist: *Yat Ji Kyun* "Sun-Character Fist"
A fist with knuckles held in a vertical line, thumb facing upward. The name refers to the resemblance the configuration has to the Chinese character for "sun."

Yu Bei: "To Prepare, Be Ready"
A call to readiness at the beginning of a set. The usual response is a bow at the waist.

[1] Zhao Da Yuan, *Practical Chin Na, A detailed analysis of the art of seizing and locking*, (Highview Press, 1993).
[2] Ching, Gene, *Bak Sil Lum vs. Shaolin Temple #2: Who's got the real Shaolin kung fu*, (Kungfu Magazine, 2001).
[3] Klingborg, Brian, *The Secrets of Northern Shaolin Kung Fu*, (Charles E. Tuttle Publishing, 1988).